SURVIVING THE CREATIVE SPACE

SURVIVING THE CREATIVE SPACE

Teamwork Techniques for Designers

Sherry Freyermuth

BLOOMSBURY VISUAL ARTS
LONDON • NEW YORK • OXFORD • NEW DELHI • SYDNEY

BLOOMSBURY VISUAL ARTS
Bloomsbury Publishing Plc
50 Bedford Square, London, WC1B 3DP, UK
1385 Broadway, New York, NY 10018, USA
29 Earlsfort Terrace, Dublin 2, Ireland

BLOOMSBURY, BLOOMSBURY VISUAL ARTS and the Diana logo are trademarks of Bloomsbury Publishing Plc

First published in Great Britain 2022

Copyright © Bloomsbury, 2022

Sherry Freyermuth has asserted her right under the Copyright, Designs and Patents Act, 1988, to be identified as Author of this work.

For legal purposes the Acknowledgments on p. 117 constitute an extension of this copyright page.

Cover image courtesy of Pexels
Cover design by Sherry Freyermuth

All rights reserved. No part of this publication may be reproduced or transmitted in any form or by any means, electronic or mechanical, including photocopying, recording, or any information storage or retrieval system, without prior permission in writing from the publishers.

Bloomsbury Publishing Plc does not have any control over, or responsibility for, any third-party websites referred to or in this book. All internet addresses given in this book were correct at the time of going to press. The author and publisher regret any inconvenience caused if addresses have changed or sites have ceased to exist, but can accept no responsibility for any such changes.

A catalogue record for this book is available from the British Library.

A catalog record for this book is available from the Library of Congress.

ISBN: PB: 978-1-350040-50-2
ePDF: 978-1-350040-51-9
eBook: 978-1-350040-52-6

Typeset by RefineCatch Limited, Bungay, Suffolk
Printed and bound in India

To find out more about our authors and books visit www.bloomsbury.com and sign up for our newsletters.

This book is dedicated to all the art and design students I've taught throughout my career. Your questions, curiosity, and insights inspired me to write this book.

CONTENTS

Preface xi

1 SURVIVING THE CREATIVE SPACE 1

The Birth of the Creative Strategy 2
Bottom Line and the Importance of Collaboration 3
Case Study: Van Leeuwen Ice Cream: How a Fresh Design Increased Sales 4
State of the Field and the Importance of Creative Teams 9
Creative Teams Definitions 10
What Makes an Effective Creative Team 10
Diversity, Equity, and Inclusion 12
Tips and Tools for Starting a Team Project 16
Becoming an Effective Team Member 18
How to Prepare Yourself for Teamwork 20
Exercise: Mapping a Value System for Your Creative Career 20

2 AGENCY TEAMS 23

Creative Agencies Come in All Shapes and Sizes 23
Defining Creative Agencies 26
Studio 28
Marketing Agency 31
Interview: Brooke Harmon and Veda Nagpurka, OH Partners 31
Branding Agency 35
Advertising Agency 36
Case Study: Citi Bike: Collaborating on a Multifaceted Campaign 36
Consultancy 42
Production Company 43
Motion Graphics Studio 43
Animation Studio 44

State of the Agency World 45
Exercise: Interview Outside Your Scope 47

3 IN-HOUSE TEAMS 51

The Value of In-house Creative Teams 52
In-house/Agency Collaboration 53
Case Study: Inside Out Awards: Celebrating In-house Creative Work 54
Working In-house Towards a Common Goal 59
Different Kinds of In-house Work 60
Collaboration In-house—Across Teams 61
Collaboration In-house—Within Teams 62
Interview: Devin O'Bryan, IBM Design 62
Creative Workflows 64
Starting Out In-house 64
Interview: Thomas Harris and Gwendolyn Mumford, AIG Insurance 65
Challenges and Opportunities Working In-house 68
Exercise: Understanding an In-house Brand 69

4 FREELANCE TEAMS 71

Freelance Creative "Teams" 71
Different Ways to Freelance 73
Developing a Style 74
Building Connections 75
Freelance Workflows 77
Case Study: Jameson Whiskey: Collaborating as a Freelance Illustrator 78
The Art Director/Copywriter Freelance Team 84
Interview: Kristen Curtis and Aldo Arias, Only Child 85
Freelance Collectives 86
The Freelancer and Client Team 86
Freelancers Need Coaching Too 87
From Freelancer to Entrepreneur 88
The Freelance Life 89
Exercise: Examining Your Work Habits 90

5 COMMUNITY AS AN EXTENSION OF CREATIVE TEAM 93

Community as Creative Team 93
Nurture Existing Creative Community 94

Grow a Creative Community 96
 Case Study: Make a Mark: Building Community by Giving Back 100
 Embrace Mentorship 106
 Quality Connection 107
 Interview: Kathleen Shannon, Co-author of *Being Boss* 108
 Community Lasts a Career 109
 Exercise: Finding a Creative Mentor 110

Conclusion 113
 Junior Espinoza's Tips for Emerging Designers 113

Acknowledgments 117
Further Reading 119
Notes 121
Index 129

PREFACE

As a graphic design professor, I often talk with my students about professional practices and life after graduation. I like to ask about their career goals and where they see themselves working in the future. Students frequently find the agency world of design "sexier" and more appealing creatively than working in-house, or, despite a limited understanding of developing a freelance practice, they romanticize what it would mean to be their own boss. Because I only have experience on in-house creative teams, I find these assumptions both intriguing and alarming. I loved both my experiences working for in-house creative teams, one as part of a three-person team in a non-profit agency designing for the city of Boston, Massachusetts, and the other as part of a large, 80+-person in-house advertising agency for Discovery Communication (now Discovery Inc.), the media power house that owns Discovery Channel, TLC, Science Channel, and Animal Planet. These were drastically different environments with very different responsibilities, and I grew significantly in each role. If I hadn't been open to working in-house, I would have missed out on two excellent job opportunities that have come to shape much of my creative work and collaborative skills today.

Widespread assumptions and misconceptions about different creative team environments prompted me to write this book, *Surviving the Creative Space*. In it, I introduce readers to the various types of creative teams and dissect what the successful ones are doing well, so that emerging professionals can use this book as a guide to help navigate the tricky space where creative output is monetized. How is creative work completed effectively without losing inspiration, spirit, and the love of design? How does collaboration and creativity happen under the pressures of efficiency? How does communication work best among creative teams? What can you do to become an invaluable member of your creative team? Through case studies and interviews, it is my hope to offer answers to these questions, and allow readers an insider's look at successful creative teams in the agency, in-house, and freelance worlds of design. Though many of the featured professionals have since changed positions or shifted the direction of their creative careers, teamwork remains essential to their practice, as it will be for you as you enter the professional design world.

1 SURVIVING THE CREATIVE SPACE

Many aspiring designers begin their career by building strong portfolios and focusing on their own individual development as a creative professional. Getting a job in design, advertising, or any other creative field does require strong craftsmanship and a command of industry-leading tools, and the importance of a strong portfolio cannot be understated. But this common approach overlooks a crucial aspect of design-world success. It overlooks the importance of understanding collaboration and teamwork. How is teamwork structured in different types of creative teams? What skills are required to be a great teammate? How can a reliable mentor transform creative development and open up new professional opportunities?

Surviving the Creative Space: Teamwork Techniques for Designers is a guide for emerging creative professionals in the early stages of their career. This book offers readers practical examples of teamwork structures in creative fields such as advertising, graphic design, motion design, and marketing. It provides a deep look into the structures of agency teams, in-house creative teams, and freelance teams, and offers tips for cultivating a rich creative community to enrich your creative life and foster professional connections.

Collaboration underlies the best creative work, and this book provides advice and exercises to help readers understand their own teamwork habits and develop skills to become strong collaborators. By learning how creative teams work and how to work effectively within them, you will become better at sharing ideas, incorporating feedback, and developing skills to persuasively present work.

Collaboration isn't only a key tool for improving creative work. It's also key for getting creative work. Oftentimes creative professionals at the junior level don't get the most creative projects until they've proven their ability to complete more basic tasks, make deadlines, and understand the work culture and dynamics of the creative team. The better a person is at adapting to their role on the team, the more responsibilities they'll be given and the faster they'll be able to advance within the team structure.

Designer Michael Bierut describes what makes creative teams unique: "I think that creative people have an interesting tension between the individual (each person's unique artistic vision) and the collective (the goals that can only be achieved through collaboration)."[1] Being able to navigate between one's individual creative voice and the collective goals of a team in order to bring an idea to life is a key component of success on a creative team.

Creative teams are important because their work impacts behavior, culture, attitudes, and opinions. The subjective nature of creative work makes it challenging to nail down the value a creative team can bring to an organization. When thinking of creative work, some people may envision a lone artist toiling away in their studio, but the reality is very different. As designer and educator Aggie Toppins has observed, focusing on individual creation is not an accurate way to understand design artifacts and learn about design processes.[2] Creative work has always been collaborative. For instance, before the introduction of computers, graphic designers relied on typesetters and printers to bring their work to life on paper. The focus on individual creative genius portrayed in graphic design history ignores the larger context of social and historical influence and the combined labor put into these works. "Many prominent designers, even if gifted leaders, were supported by teams who created value for their businesses," writes Toppins. "Individual creators are, to no small extent, historical fabrications."[3] Today, as in the past, creative work always involves creative teams.

The Birth of the Creative Strategy

> Is creativity some obscure esoteric art form? Not on your life. It's the most practical thing a business man can employ.
>
> **BILL BERNBACH**[4]

Advertising pioneer Bill Bernbach's claim that creativity is essentially practical offers insight into creativity's value today. While many people perceive the creative professional to be driven by whim and intuition, creativity is in fact a professional tool that requires discipline—the discipline to harness one's imagination.

Bernbach was part of a mid-twentieth-century advertising agency, Doyle Dane Bernbach, that revolutionized how creative teams function. In the early years of advertising, teamwork was much different than we know it today. It functioned more like an assembly line in a factory where a client would hire the advertising company, the boss would tell the copywriter to write the copy, the graphic designer would make a design and put together a mechanical that incorporated the copy, and, once approved, the design was off to the printer. While there were teams of people working to make the creative work come to life, each team was siloed in their own area of expertise and they weren't working together to develop ideas. Bernbach's firm brought the copywriters together with the designers and art directors to collaborate on their concepts. This allowed them to develop strong strategies to create more thoughtful and innovative solutions for advertisements. "If two good creative people get together, an art director and a copywriter, sometimes you don't know who's writing the copy and who's doing the art because you get excited about the thought," said Bernbach in 1971, reflecting on his collaborations with Paul Rand at the Weintraub advertising agency.[5] For Bernbach, this was the important thing. This model changed the way advertising and design teams are structured. Now, the art director–copywriter team is commonplace. Creative teams were always important for design, but now creatives with different backgrounds and expertise work together more intimately.

Bottom Line and the Importance of Collaboration

Bernbach is remembered not only for his agency's innovative approach, which changed team structures within advertising. He's also remembered for great campaigns for brands like Volkswagen, Life Cereal, and Polaroid. The success of these campaigns translated into increased revenue for the companies, thus showing that good advertising is good for business in many ways, including helping to increase the bottom line. Today, design more broadly is increasingly understood as having the power to drive business forward.

To measure this power, Jeneanne Rae and the Design Management Institute have developed the Design Value Index (DVI) to quantify the value of design thinking for organizations. The most recent study shows that over a ten-year period, "design-led companies have maintained significant stock market advantage, outperforming the S&P by an extraordinary 211%."[6] While Rae acknowledges that many stakeholders within an organization understand the value of design, quantifying it can help justify larger investments in design within an organization. "Those most interested in quantifying the value of design are the financial people," she writes, "many don't really understand the power of design and what it can do for brand equity, customer satisfaction, mitigating competitive threats or building loyalty."[7] The DVI showcases how companies that embrace design will grow faster and earn more, making a strong case for the value of all organizations to make intentional decisions about design.

This value exceeds monetary value, as shown in the case of Vanessa Dewey at Mattel. Dewey was a team member of the packaging design team at Mattel, where she made innovative package design solutions for beloved brands such as Barbie and Toy Story. While Dewey was able to innovate and develop her skills, she felt a need to refuel her creativity and find new inspiration. By engaging in her creative community through conference events, she came up with the idea to develop a speaker series at Mattel that would inspire creatives. By speaking up about her ideas and pushing leaders at Mattel to think about creative impact at an organizational level, Dewey became the first Lead in Creative and Development

Experience, shifting from the design team to HR team, where she "defied stereotypes by bringing a creative, human-centered design approach to a traditionally corporate department."[8] Her creative role became further-reaching, by making creativity part of the culture in all parts of the "house" at Mattel.

Angelica McKinley can speak firsthand about the impact of design within an organization. As an art director for print at the *New York Times*, in 2012, she could see that things were changing in the 150-year-old organization. When John Branch's multimedia piece "Snow Fall: The Avalanche at Tunnel Creek" went live on December 20, 2012, it gained fast attention for its still-photo slide shows, animated simulations, and aerial video, which were recognized with a Peabody Award and a Pulitzer in Featured Writing.[9] McKinley describes how suddenly designers had more input at meetings, and writers wanted to know how they, too, could collaborate with the design team to make their writing stand out in the rapidly expanding digital landscape. McKinley made a quick study of the changes happening around her, and she wanted to be part of the new digital space in reporting. She learned everything she could about digital and in 2015 made the leap from the print team to the digital design team, where she collaborated with writers to create digital content for the paper's website and social media channels. As the *New York Times* and other papers have continued to develop their online presence, design has become an increasingly important part of the company's operations. To bolster readers' understanding of a story, designers like McKinley work with writers, programmers, photographers, and other media creators. Design success depends on collaboration.[10]

Collaboration is key to a lasting career in creative industries, and understanding the inner workings of creative teams will aid you on your journey as you work to *survive the creative space*.

CASE STUDY: VAN LEEUWEN ICE CREAM: HOW A FRESH DESIGN INCREASED SALES

Great design happens when teams foster strong collaboration. In this case study, the value of design is evident through increased sales after a rebranding project.

Project
Brand identity and packaging redesign

Client
Van Leeuwen Ice Cream

Creative Team
Agency: Pentagram
Office: New York
Project lead: Natasha Jen
Project team: Joseph Han, Ji Park, Rhea Manglapus, Georgina McDonald

Duration
2017

Description
The project focused on new packaging, because this is the first touch point a customer will see when deciding whether to buy the ice cream.

Process
Natasha Jen and her team at Pentagram redesigned the packaging for Van Leeuwen Ice Cream, a company based in New York and Los Angeles. The team worked closely with the founders of the company to develop the project.[11] They used a color palette inspired by ice cream, and refined the packaging's primary focus: the logo. The design team applied the design system to additional brand materials including ice cream trucks, stores, gift cards, uniforms, and stationery. The resulting cheerful and distinct design increased brand recognition.

Outcome
After the launch of the new identity system and package design, sales for Van Leeuwen Ice Cream increased by 50 percent, proving that investing in design can yield a positive financial impact on an organization.[12]

Questions for Thought
What aspect of the rebrand do you think had the most impact on the increased sales? Was it the packaging? The in-store design? The cohesive approach to the brand system?

What other brands do you think could benefit from a redesign?

FIGURE 1.1 Identity.

The updated Van Leeuwen logo keeps the original wordmark but refines the typography to give the logo more prominence.

FIGURE 1.2 Business cards.

The Van Leeuwen business cards and packaging utilize a color palette inspired by ice cream.

FIGURE 1.3 Tubs.

The minimal package design reflects the purity of the product ingredients and is unified across every ice cream line. The distinctive color palette also helps consumers identify flavors easily.

FIGURE 1.4 Van.

The Van Leeuwen brand is also translated to their ice cream truck design.

SURVIVING THE CREATIVE SPACE

FIGURE 1.5 Window.

Window signage is clean and inviting, allowing passersby to see customers enjoying the product inside.

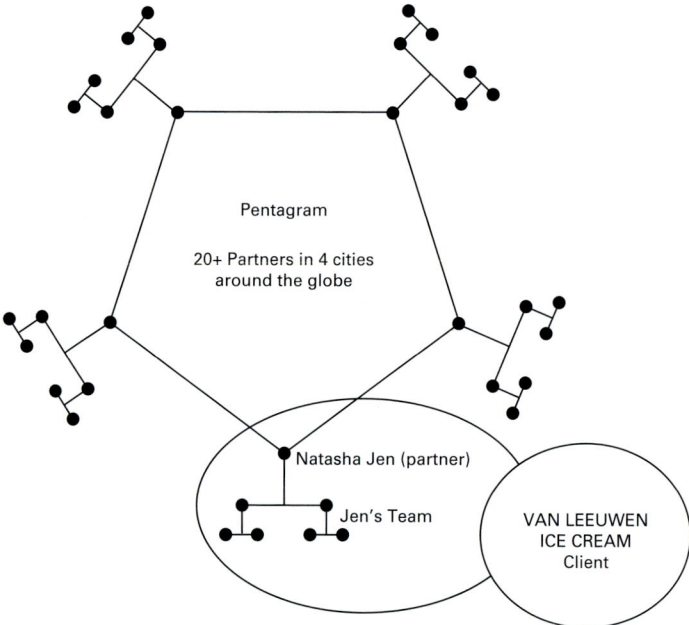

FIGURE 1.6 Organizational chart for the Van Leeuwen brand identity project.

This chart details the creative team organizational structure for the Van Leeuwen brand identity project led by Natasha Jen. Pentagram uses a pod agency team structure and designers often engage directly with clients rather than working with an account manager (see Chapter 2 for more information on agency structures).

8   SURVIVING THE CREATIVE SPACE

State of the Field and the Importance of Creative Teams

> **A new design paradigm**—Much of the work in solving problems at the systems level is in analysis and planning, not in physical production. It is distributed across experts from a variety of disciplines with different worldviews who work closely as a team.
>
> **MEREDITH DAVIS**[13]

What shape will creative teams take in the coming years? What design skills will be most useful for helping organizations improve their bottom line? To answer these and other questions, AIGA, the professional association for design, partnered with design educator and researcher Meredith Davis to examine the state of design today. The outcome is the "Design Futures" report, which examines what skills are going to be most relevant for students to learn and what jobs will be most prevalent for designers in the years to come.[14]

The report recognizes that although creative work in the twentieth century was always collaborative in nature, it was based on an industrial age perspective wherein designers valued an object-driven process. This means designers would problem solve within a form-giving context such as creating a magazine publication, an advertisement, or product packaging. Higher education reflected these challenges by teaching principles of visual abstraction and technical mastery of typography, layout, photography, etc. and then moving into assignments that gave students opportunities to demonstrate these form-giving skills necessary to get jobs in publishing, print advertising, and other physical media.

This began to change in the 1980s with the introduction of the personal computer. But it was during the following decade, just before the new millennium, that design work transformed. Computer technology became sophisticated enough to do the kind of tasks previously done by the skilled hands of typesetters and production artists creating mechanicals and paste-ups of design layouts. Designers were increasingly in demand to create websites. And yet even as the work changed, the mentality remained the same. During the dot-com boom of the late 1990s, web designers adhered to the object-driven principle; once a website was complete, it didn't really change much.

But the way we use digital technology today, in the 2020s, has transformed this mindset. We are living in a "knowledge economy" where economic growth is more dependent on access to information than the production of goods. Approximately half the world's population owns a personal computer in the form of a smartphone, and they use it to access information.[15] People interact online using social media platforms, and service-driven companies like Amazon and Uber do not produce goods for customers but instead create easy-to-use digital platforms to facilitate experiences. Rather than relying on intuition, designers now have to think more about human-centered outcomes that are based on research and observation. Results are no longer perfect objects, but experiences that evolve. A "good enough for now" mindset allows for faster delivery to market for design solutions. But fast delivery requires collaboration.

The "Design Futures" report indicates that in the twenty-first century, emerging creative professionals need to embrace ambiguity, complex problems and systems thinking, and group decision-making processes. Though creative teams have a long history, they are uniquely important today, and will continue to evolve in unforeseen ways.

Creative Teams Definitions

Creative teams can work in many different ways, and this book addresses three of the most common creative team structures.

Agency

In this book, the term agency is used broadly to define companies that work for external clients to deliver creative work. Agencies build collaborative creative teams with roles such as art director, copywriter, and strategist to deliver creative work to improve the communication needs of an organization. There are several business models and terms for agencies, and these will be explored in more detail throughout Chapter 2.

In-house

In-house creative teams have a supportive role within an organization by providing many of the same creative services an agency would provide, but team members work internally as employees of the organization. Chapter 3 focuses specifically on the unique features of in-house creative team structures.

Freelance

Freelance creative professionals provide creative services to clients, but work independently to find clients and complete projects. Sometimes freelancers team up on a per project basis. The dynamics of freelance creative teams are explained in Chapter 4.

What Makes an Effective Creative Team

Though this book will introduce you to many creative professionals who have different experiences with, perspectives on, and insights into creative teams, there are three fundamental pillars to effective creative teams. They are:

- Creative safety
- Diversity, equity, and inclusion
- Clear communication and expectations

Creative Safety

To achieve success, team members must feel safe and supported. When Google analyzed what makes the perfect team, research showed that it wasn't about a perfect formula of personality types, but instead psychological safety. When team members had interpersonal trust and mutual respect, each team member felt supported and that they could make mistakes without repercussions.[16] If team members feel like they can't make mistakes, then it's hard to take risks and achieve innovative and creative results.

But creative safety isn't a given. Creative director Ramona Todoca remembers discussing the importance of creative trust and chemistry with a colleague who was wrestling with a hiring decision:

> We were in the office super late and he had just interviewed a designer. He asked me and another colleague if we would hire someone that we really liked and is easy to work with who had an okay but not extraordinary portfolio, or someone extraordinary who it just didn't feel like we jived with. He was in a real pickle because he felt that both avenues were valid and both candidates could be great for the job. Our colleague said, "Look it's 11:30 p.m. and we're hanging out here and doing work. We spend so much time together, more time than with our significant others. At the end of the day, you're going to spend so much time with the person you hire. You might as well enjoy their company and feel inspired by them."

When a team has good chemistry, both intellectually and creatively, it paves the road to be comfortable enough to throw out ideas even if it makes you feel vulnerable.[17]

Diversity, Equity, and Inclusion

Diverse teams make better decisions. In a recent study, researchers examined 566 business decisions that were made by teams from different companies. The research concluded that homogeneous, all-male teams made the right decision 58 percent of the time. When gender diversity was added to the team make-up, decision making improved and the team made the right decision 73 percent of the time. When teams were diversified in terms of gender and age, better decision making increased to 80 percent. Finally, the study tested diversity in terms of gender, age, and geography. These highly diverse teams were most successful of all, with better decision making increasing to 87 percent, giving diverse teams a 29 percent increase in better decision making compared with homogeneous teams.[18] These results suggest that diversity, equity, and inclusion are crucial considerations for successful creative teams. But what exactly do these frequently used terms mean?

DIVERSITY, EQUITY, AND INCLUSION

Here are some useful definitions, borrowed from the Creative Reaction Lab Field Guide:[19]

Diversity: Diversity is when there is a variety of characteristics within a group, such as a neighborhood, school, community, or city. Diversity is defined by a variety of identifiers and characteristics that, in the case of people, reflect our individuality. However, definitions of diversity are often limited and largely confined to visible aspects such as race, age, or gender rather than less visible aspects such as ability status, nationality, or mental well-being. When we say that a group of people is diverse, we mean that the people that make up the group represent different backgrounds, perspectives, and life experiences.

Inclusion: Inclusion is the leveraging of difference by integrating diverse perspectives and creating a better outcome for all. Inclusion is an invitation that not only accepts differences, but celebrates and embeds them.

Note: Diversity and inclusion are not interchangeable. There can be diversity without inclusion and inclusion without diversity.

Equity: Equity revolves around systemic outcomes and exists when outcomes are no longer predicted by any aspect of an individual's identity.

Equality: Equality is the basic need of being equal, especially in status, rights, and opportunities.

Social scientist Sarah Saska, whose research focuses on equity, technology, and innovation, draws the following important distinction between equity and equality:

> While often used interchangeably, equity and equality mean different things and lead to different results. When we treat everyone equally, we treat everyone the same, but when we treat everyone equitably, we focus on individualistic needs. In a diverse workplace, differences exist, and people require support in different ways. Equity asks us to acknowledge that everyone has different needs, experiences, and opportunities.
>
> People from marginalized groups often have more barriers to overcome when accessing resources and opportunities than those from dominant or more privileged groups. In a diverse organization, equity-inspired design identifies barriers and inequities and helps to elevate the people on the margins to an equal playing field.[20]

What do these concepts mean for creative teams? Here is an illustrative example:

- **Diversity is where everyone on the team, with their own unique perspective, is invited to the meeting.**
- **Equity means that everyone on the team gets to contribute ideas to the brainstorming session in their preferred format (written, verbal, etc.).**
- **Inclusion means that everyone feels their ideas are valued by the team.**

> While academia and the design industry have tried to become more accepting in recent years, there is much work to be done to make these spaces more inclusive. Representation matters ... Calling out the fact that design has the capacity to be an exclusive space that does not always value, respect or celebrate our identities is critical to name.
>
> **KELLY WALTERS**[21]

Working on a diverse team can be difficult, because people come from different backgrounds and don't necessarily share perspectives. This challenge is actually a benefit for creative teams, because a multitude of perspectives means myriad opportunities to see the project in new ways. A creative team will benefit from diversity, equity, and inclusion because they can help foster a wider range of ideas and thus more creative solutions for clients.

While there are challenges to working on a diverse team, if you focus on building trust and empathy with one another, the team can achieve great results. Team members can facilitate inclusion by practicing a "visible commitment" to diversity, "humility," "awareness of personal bias," "curiosity" and empathy towards others, "cultural intelligence," and "effective collaboration" that focuses on empowering others and team cohesion.[22] Awareness of personal bias and cultural intelligence are the concepts that require the most self-awareness in this list. Bias is a tendency to believe one's views are better or more favorable than others. Awareness of personal bias requires someone to acknowledge that their personal views are subjective and shaped by their own personal experiences. Understanding this in a professional setting allows colleagues with different experiences to be more open-minded to differing opinions and beliefs. Similarly, cultural intelligence is a skill whereby someone can work effectively in culturally diverse situations. Cultural experiences inform a person's worldview, which requires an open mind to navigate the differing viewpoints within a diverse team setting. In the book *Intercultural Collaboration by Design*, the authors explain that "when teams understand how best to communicate with each other, respect each other's work habits, and create opportunities for everyone to communicate, their diversity functions as an asset that facilitates shared outcomes."[23] To better understand how your actions are impacting the team, it can be helpful to seek feedback from a trusted advisor. Ask them to observe you and then schedule a time to discuss what they saw. A proactive approach to improving inclusivity and diversity will enhance organizational culture and allow for greater team success.

Clear Communication and Expectations

For a creative team to be effective, each team member must understand their role and responsibilities and be able to communicate with the other members of the team. This clarity helps facilitate accountability so projects can run smoothly. The success of each individual results in success for the team.

Processes and routines should be documented and shared with new members of a team. For instance, in a large advertising agency, a junior designer might have to go through several rounds of approval before submitting a design. After receiving an assignment, they might have to take the following steps to complete a project:

1. An account manager brings a job to the team and it's assigned to a junior designer.
   a. Ask questions—check with account managers for details from the client and ask the art director for creative insight.
2. Complete the first draft.
3. Get feedback from the team.
4. Send to copy editor for proofing.

5 Revise and send back for team feedback and proofing.*
6 Send revised project to the art director for approval.
7 Send to the account manager for client approval.
8 Manage the files for print or digital output.
9 Double check the specs (i.e., height and width, image resolution, color management, etc.) for accuracy.
10 Submit for print or digital publication.

This long list of processes may not be intuitive to a new team member, particularly if this is their first time working on a larger agency team. If a team hasn't developed a clear list of procedures, a new team member might overlook or bypass important steps. In a situation where workflow processes are unclear, ask for clear instructions, write them down, and keep the list as a reference. Better yet, share the guidelines with new team members. This will benefit everyone as the junior designer moves up and helps on-board the next new team member.

Brainstorming is another process that can benefit from a more structured approach. Time and again, research has shown that group brainstorming generates fewer innovative ideas than when people brainstorm individually and then gather as a group to exchange their ideas. This is because people tend to feel social pressure to conform to the group, thus generating fewer original ideas.[24] It helps to develop strategies where participants have the opportunity to work alone before converging their ideas as a group.[25] Another helpful strategy when working in a large group of over ten people is to break down into several smaller groups of about five to ten people per group and then conduct brainstorming activities. It's also useful to switch up groups after a session to help combat group think and allow for new creative ideas to form. Many design thinking workshops use permanent markers and sticky notes. Writing with a dark black marker on a small piece of notepaper has a few benefits. First, it makes it so no one can write too much, erase, or get too particular about an idea. By writing one idea per piece of paper, the notes can be moved around to bridge ideas and forge new connections. The common use of the black marker signifies that each team member's voice carries equal weight regardless of how loud their actual voice is within the session.

Enabling clear communication and expectations is vital for a creative team to succeed. While it's important for leaders to exhibit these skills, each team member must also work to develop clear communication strategies and facilitate open lines of communication with all members of the team.

---

*Sometimes a project goes through many rounds of revisions and proofing. The best way to cut down on the revision loop is to develop a strong attention to detail and listen closely to feedback; however, some projects just take longer to get right and that's okay too.

> ## TIPS AND TOOLS FOR STARTING A TEAM PROJECT
>
> **Hopes and Fears Design Thinking Activity**
> The IBM Design Thinking Field Guide provides numerous activities that can help facilitate teamwork. The Hopes and Fears activity is particularly helpful at the beginning of a new project: "If you're starting a project, kicking-off a workshop, or bringing in new team members, this activity helps you get to know each other, expose aspirations and concerns, and prepare everyone to start."[26]
>
> **Creating a Community Agreement**
> Work with your team to develop a community agreement about how you'd like to work. It's important the whole team contributes as opposed to being conceived by the supervisor. The National Equity Project has resources for developing a community agreement, and using them can help a group of people form into a true team: "The process of constructing agreements is often more important than the product. Agreements come from a consensus-driven process to identify what every person in the group needs from each other and commits to each other to feel safe, supported, open and trusting."[27]

Team Members

Just as there are many different kinds of creative teams, there are also many different positions within a creative team. Teams are made up of creative roles and management roles, and how they collaborate varies based on the organizational structure of the company. There are many different job titles available across creative industries, and this is just a small list of common team member job titles:

Creative Team Roles
Creative Director—Creative directors are upper-level management. Their role is often to sign off on and approve final creative work. Larger creative organizations may employ several creative directors to oversee a particular team or client account. An executive creative director is the top-level position within a creative team. An associate creative director is another level of management, and they would report to the creative director. Creative directors tend to meet with clients,

collaborate with the account management team to acquire new business, and focus on big-picture projects within an organization.

Art Director—Art directors usually oversee a small team or collaborate with a partner to develop creative work. They often work on both creative and strategy and have more responsibilities and access to clients than junior level team members. Art directors can have a background in design or copywriting or other creative area, depending on the needs of the team and the larger organization. Art directors may also supervise and delegate to junior level team members.

Designer/Copywriter—Designers and copywriters follow a similar hierarchy of junior level, mid-level, senior, and associate, depending on the team's structure. Designers and copywriters usually report to art directors to develop creative work. At the junior level, they are often tasked with a smaller aspect of a project to assist the team in meeting deadlines and goals, while a senior level copywriter will likely have more responsibility for the strategic vision of a project.

Intern—Interns are usually students or recent graduates providing support for a creative team on a temporary and often part-time basis. When seeking internships, it's important to look for opportunities with organizations that value the process of learning. Interns should be paid for their work, and unpaid opportunities should be scrutinized.[28]

While job titles are important—particularly when it comes to compensation and hierarchy—it's also important to understand that job titles may mean different things at different organizations. For example, it could be that the art director and designer positions at two different companies are actually quite similar in terms of workload and responsibilities.

Management team member roles

Creative teams are not made up only of creatives. Often, they include members whose roles focus on project management and client relations. The job titles may vary depending on the industry, but common positions include:

Account Manager—Account managers are skilled communicators who develop client relations and work as mediator between the client and the creative team, freeing up time for the creatives to focus on creative work rather than client communications. Account managers often collaborate with art directors and creative directors to develop project timelines and manage client expectations.

Project Manager—Project managers sometimes play a similar role to account managers, interfacing with clients. But in other cases, they focus more on project organization and scheduling. This requires a comprehensive understanding of creative processes and task workflows in order to help establish a realistic schedule and help keep the team on track to complete on time. Project managers might also be in charge of managing a project budget.

Producer—A producer usually oversees projects for television, motion design, or animation. They handle many aspects of a motion project such as budgets, contracts, managing the project schedule, and client relations.

Scrum Master—User experience design teams often include a scrum master, whose primary responsibility is to maintain the team process by protecting it from outside distractions, facilitating communication, and helping it strategize and meet deadlines.

> An effective team has people with different skills and responsibilities, and if everybody comes to the team with the same resources then it's not very effective.
> **ELLEN LUPTON**[29]

Becoming an Effective Team Member

At this point it should be clear that creative teams are complex organisms. What can you do to contribute positively to an effective creative team? The four most important attributes individuals can bring to their work on a team are:

- Reliability
- Strong communication
- Commitment to the team's success
- Initiative

Reliability is crucial for building trust among team members. In the book *Intercultural Collaboration by Design*, authors Denielle J. Emans and Kelly M. Murdoch-Kitt showcase the importance of trust for successful teamwork. "When it comes to building trust," they write, "delivering on promises and tasks, or personal accountability, is another driving force for successful teamwork."[30] One way to establish trust is to prove accountability by showing up and delivering work on time. When team members understand their role on the team and what others expect, it's easier to fulfill that role and showcase accountability. It's okay to be vulnerable on a team and ask questions or admit when you don't understand something. Trust can be established by admitting to yourself and to others that you don't have the answer and proactively seeking help.

Strong communication skills are another important key to successful participation on a team. When the Carnegie Institute of Technology researched their own organization's success, they found that 85 percent of it was "due to skills in 'human engineering', personality, and ability to communicate, negotiate, and lead." A mere 15 percent owed to technical ability. This means that "people skills or skills highly related to emotional intelligence were crucial skills."[31] Excellent communication strategy is not simply agreeing with other members of the team. Rather, it involves building enough trust and mutual respect to critique and respectfully disagree with one another. Equity designer Antoinette Carroll says it's important to surround yourself with people who challenge you, because when it does eventually happen it can be a culture shock if you're not used to it. "I would argue that any group you're a part of, make sure you have people that challenge you at the same time and not just agree with everything that you say."[32]

Good communication is especially important today, as teams in creative fields are becoming more interdisciplinary and, as a result, differing views are more common. As the "Design Futures" report explains, "Anthropologists, psychologists, computer scientists, cultural theorists, business strategists, data scientists, and other specialists now participate in the development of design solutions."[33] Coming from different fields, these people speak different languages specific to their area of expertise. Great communication skills are especially important so that team members can convey their specialized knowledge to the rest of the team and facilitate understanding. It's important to develop ways to talk across different disciplines so everyone is having the same conversation.

While personal success can motivate job performance, an effective team requires that its members demonstrate a **commitment to the team's success**. As designer Ellen Lupton says, "being on a team you have to give up ownership of your piece of it. And you know in a team project everybody's contributing ideas to one pot. There's no winner."[34] Being part of a team requires putting aside personal interests and making sure work serves the good of the project so that the team can deliver the best creative work for the client. IBM Design director, Devin O'Bryan developed recommendations for seven core habits to help all members stay committed to the success of the team:[35]

1. Empathy: the drive to understand what makes others tick, honor their perspectives, and do what you can to inject delight into their experiences.
2. Vulnerability: a willingness to contribute your ideas to the world, open yourself up to criticism, test your assumptions, fail early, and learn fast.
3. Curiosity: the drive to see what makes something tick. To understand why why why WHY!
4. Humility: the ability to suspend your ego, accept that you don't know everything, and invite others to share their knowledge with you.
5. Integrity: to align with your team, adapt, improvise, and be transparent about your failures as well as your successes—in the interest of good work.

6 Flexibility: to be open to new ideas, willing to compromise, and able to build a better solution through embracing constraints.

7 Audacity: to dive into challenges with enthusiasm and be willing to ask for forgiveness instead of permission.

Taking **initiative** is another key part of becoming a great team member. Leadership is not just for senior designers, art directors, and creative directors. Team members can cultivate creative leadership skills by being proactive and empathetic; responding to the group's needs while meeting the client's demands; and establishing a future vision rather than just a reactionary approach to the work and thinking long term about the success of the group. Focusing on execution will only take you so far, whereas leadership and communication will let you advance much further in your career. No matter where you are in your career, you can adopt this mindset. Remember that soft skills are as important—if not more important—than tech skills.

How to Prepare Yourself for Teamwork

> Employees are more productive and pay more attention to company profit when they are working for something they believe in, are treated with respect, and are well-paid.
>
> **MEREDITH DAVIS**[36]

One way to identify the role you can play on a creative team is by thinking about your own priorities and values. Consider your current habits and future goals as a creative professional. It's helpful to reflect on your own core values to guide your role on a team in the creative space.

EXERCISE: MAPPING A VALUE SYSTEM FOR YOUR CREATIVE CAREER

In this exercise, you will explore the core values that guide your creative outlook. Start by drawing a mind map with your name in the center and four points out from that center. In each circle write the following: Collaboration, Communication, Culture, and Lifestyle. From each of the four circles, write three words in separate circles to represent your values for each category.

Collaboration: What do you value about collaboration? Do you prefer to go it alone, or do you like working on a team to meet your goals? Write three words that describe your teamwork style and collaborative values. Words to consider: alignment, agility, authenticity, commitment, dependability, efficiency, fearlessness, good humor, honesty, independence, leadership, open-mindedness, perseverance, positivity

Communication: What do you value about communication? What's your communication style? Do you prefer to work alone or talk through challenges with a trusted collaborator? Write three words that describe your values about communication.
Words to consider: awareness, authority, balance, calmness, candor, clarity, connection, cooperation, consistency, credibility, decisiveness, enthusiasm, empathy, humility

Culture: What type of work culture do you value? Do like a fast-paced environment or do you prefer having time to think through a challenge? Do you like balancing multiple projects or do you want the opportunity to do a deep dive on a single project at a time? Do you like an open office setting or would you rather work remotely? Write three words that describe your values about culture.
Words to consider: ambition, belonging, comfort, creativity, discovery, diversity, freedom, fun, generosity, innovation, kindness, motivation

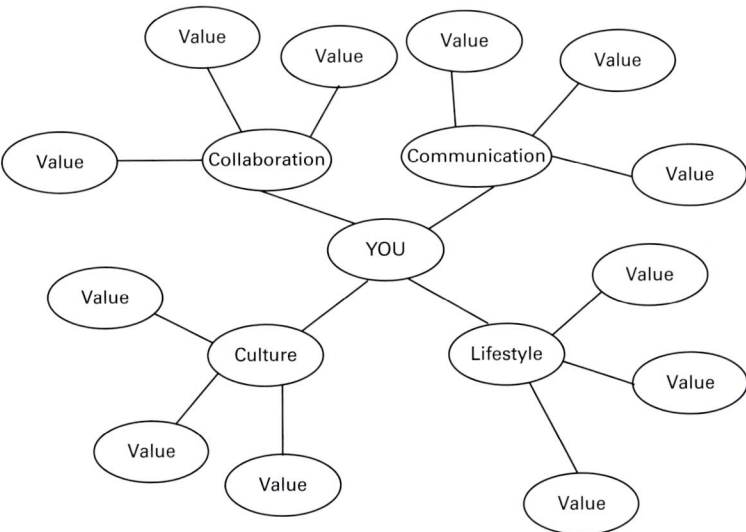

FIGURE 1.7 Mapping a value system.
This diagram serves as a template for how you can map your own value system utilizing a mind map structure.

Lifestyle: What do you value outside of work? How do you want to spend your time outside of work? Is it location-specific? Does it require a particular schedule? Would a flexible schedule allow you to reach your personal goals or is it increased financial compensation that you require? Write three words that describe your values about lifestyle.
Words to consider: adventure, balance, choice, control, curiosity, education, energy, entertainment, family, growth, health, humor, individuality, joy, liberation, passion

Once you map your twelve words, try to find and draw the connections between them. Develop these words into three to five statements about your values.

Example:
I value dependable collaboration, clear communication, and a generous work culture. I want to work for a team that embodies these traits and values my commitment to family.

2 AGENCY TEAMS

In February 2017, Allyson Lack stood before an audience packed with eager designers waiting for the main event: to hear from renowned designer Paula Scher. As a successful female creative business owner herself, Lack was honored to introduce her personal design hero. In 1991, Scher became the first female partner at Pentagram, the world-renowned design studio with offices in four different cities across Europe and North America. Scher's career path served as a model for Lack, who sought to lead her own design studio in a field still dominated by men. In the early stages of her career, it was important to Lack have someone to look up to. "Seeing Paula as a pioneer at Pentagram with her own dedicated team stood as a beacon," she announced to the crowd, "always a reminder that it was feasible and attainable."[1] Lack attributes the success of her business, Principle, to leaders like Scher who forged the way for up-and-coming women in the industry.

Lack founded Principle with two other women, all of whom were freelancing in different cities. They saw Pentagram as a premier example of designers working in a multi-city format and wanted to create a similar team structure that would allow them to partner and collaborate despite being separated by geography. Lack has described the arrangement's unintentional advantages. "Our website looked like we were much bigger than we were (*offices in three cities!*) so we landed much bigger gigs than we ever thought possible ... within a couple of months, we had contracts with Microsoft, Nordstrom, and Chronicle Books among others."[2] The team structure at Principle was different because each partner operated under their own LLC. Even though there are similarities between the two agencies, they operate in totally different ways. Pentagram provided the inspiration, but Principle forged their own path.

Creative Agencies Come in All Shapes and Sizes

Creative agencies are organizations working to deliver creative projects for external clients. They can specialize in different kinds of creative work including branding, advertising, marketing strategy, design, or video production. Some studios, like Pentagram, offer a combination of specialties. Clients hire creative agencies to build brand awareness, help improve visibility or customer experience, and improve the company's bottom line. For example, a beverage company launches an exciting new flavor to their line of products. To promote sales and build brand loyalty, they would hire a creative agency to promote the new flavor and create awareness and highlight the benefits of the new product.

Creative agencies can vary widely in size. Small agencies generally have fewer than twenty employees, mid-size agencies range from twenty to fifty employees, and large agencies employ over fifty people within their organizations, but can scale much larger to hundreds or even thousands of employees. Agencies of different sizes work in different ways. For example, Principle, which began with just three partners—and, with fewer than fifteen employees, remains small even now—prides itself on having a lean and nimble team structure that provides efficient and affordable services for brands large and small.

Brand agencies come in various sizes and team structures, but typically include people working in the following roles: creative director, business director, design director, writing director, designer, copywriter, and account manager. Though small and large agencies employ people in these roles, the expectations can be very different. Lean teams often require a multifaceted skill set and the ability to take on a wider range of creative work, while larger agencies often allow for more specialization. Publicis is an example of a large advertising agency. This French multinational agency is one of the biggest in the world with over 75,000 employees across the globe.[3] While working in such a large organization might seem intimidating, the upside is that the company's global reach invites dynamic client work from large brands. Also, larger agencies offer more opportunities for career shifts within the organization than do smaller agencies, where to make a shift often requires moving on to an entirely new organization. But regardless of size, creative work at an agency requires close collaboration with a team.

In some cases, size can determine the structure of a creative agency. For instance, small agencies might choose to work within a specific industry such as real estate to help manage client growth and offer niche services that meet specialized industry needs. Large agencies might attract bigger clients by offering a full-service experience such as brand identity, advertising, and marketing strategy all in one place. Small agencies may look for multifaceted creative professionals who can step into multiple roles within a project. Large agencies might hire more specialized creatives to fill gaps in knowledge within a team.

Structures can vary widely within creative agencies, but three of the most common types are the traditional model, the matrix model, and the pod system.[4] In the traditional organizational model, the structure is highly tiered, with one central leader or leadership team. The traditional model has clear, yet sometimes rigid structures that have been criticized for being too siloed and lacking pathways for cross-team collaborations.

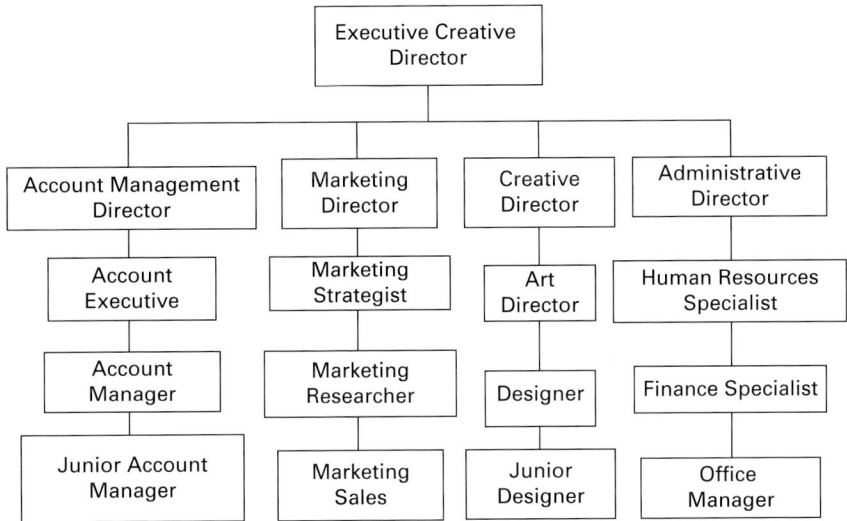

FIGURE 2.1 Traditional agency model.
The traditional agency model provides a rigid leadership structure with a clear hierarchy and management structure.

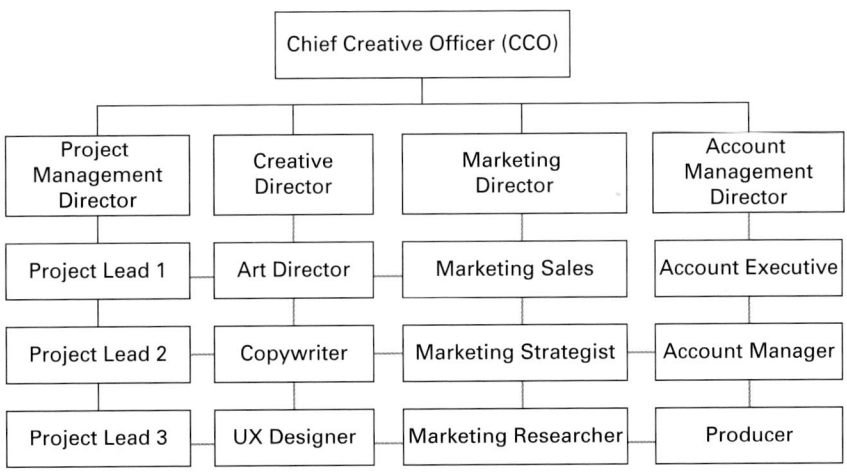

FIGURE 2.2 Matrix agency model.
The matrix agency model offers a flexible structure with team members reporting to two or more managers.

In the matrix model, the structure is based on a hierarchy similar to the traditional model, but it allows for more flexibility and interdisciplinary collaboration. This model is less siloed than the traditional model and allows for easier communication between teams. In the matrix structure, team members report to two or more managers: a functional manager who is the highest authority for decision making within the team, and a project manager who operates as a

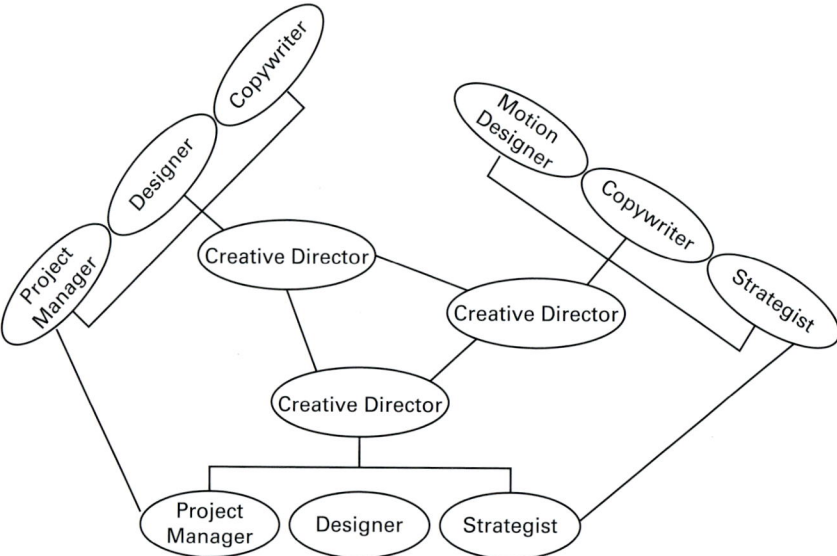

FIGURE 2.3 Pod agency model.
The pod agency model is an organic team structure with a flatter organizational structure.

secondary point of authority. One of the main benefits of this structure is a more efficient workflow, because resources and team members are shared across projects as needed. This offers dynamic and highly collaborative team structures. To be effective, matrix teams need to have clarity of team member roles within each project, and management authority must be clear in order to reduce authority confusion for team members.

In the pod system, the organizational structure is flatter than the previous two models. This structure is more organic and utilizes smaller groups with multidisciplinary team members who work together on a common goal. The client has more direct access to the team creators, and the goal is to eliminate time wasted waiting for feedback that has to go up the chain of command for approval.

There's no single best structure for an agency team, and this chapter explores a range of team styles to help an emerging professional find their best fit on a creative agency team.

DEFINING CREATIVE AGENCIES

In this chapter, the term agency is used broadly to define companies that work for external clients to deliver creative work. But there are more specific terms available to describe specific business models and agency types. Here are a few important ones that will be explored in more detail throughout this chapter.

Studio
"A studio is any interdependent group of designers who work together on and share responsibility for design projects all the way through to final handoff to production."[5]

Marketing Agency
Marketing agencies implement and manage promotional and sales strategies to achieve a client's business goals.

Branding Agency
A branding agency offers "research, planning, copywriting, implementation, and stewardship, all of which are necessary to make decisions about how a brand unfolds over time and not just what it looks like."[6]

Advertising Agency
Advertising agencies create, plan, and implement paid ad spots and sometimes other forms of promotion for their clients.

Consultancy
"A consultancy is a group that advises and coaches on design strategy and direction in a way that addresses the whole client or company, rather than focusing on a specific marketing, advertising, or product need that can be answered through a deliverable. The visuals that it produces are usually handed off for final execution to in-house design groups or external production studios."[7]

Production Company
"A production company offers production services to both studios and agencies, usually for motion graphics or large-scale digital products."[8]

Motion Graphics Studio
A motion graphics studio creates video marketing strategies for clients utilizing creative motion and animation techniques.

> **Animation Studio**
>
> Animation studios are entertainment companies that use similar tools as motion graphics studios but typically in the service of narrative series or film.
>
> For more useful industry definitions, see Juliette Cezzar's *The AIGA Guide to Careers in Graphic and Communication Design* from which many of the above definitions were taken.

Studio

Definition: "A studio is any interdependent group of designers who work together on and share responsibility for design projects all the way through to final handoff to production."[9]

Founded in 1972, Pentagram was created during the hippie era with a communal spirit in mind. The company name was inspired by the symbol of a pentagram: a five-pointed star created by drawing five continuous and connected lines, a metaphor for the agency's structure. The founders—Alan Fletcher, Theo Crosby, Colin Forbes, Kenneth Grange, and Mervyn Kurlansky—were top creative talents, well known for their work in design and advertising. Rather than organize a business with a multitiered leadership structure, they created a design studio that was organized around partnership. They designed Pentagram's structure to function more like a cooperative than a corporation.

> At Pentagram each partner shares equally in the profits.
>
> **LUKE HAYMAN**[10]

When Pentagram expanded beyond the five original founders, they decided to bring in new partners at the same level and share profits equally. As current Pentagram partner Michael Bierut puts it, this makes the studio "unique not just in design but among professional service firms in general: almost always, when profit is calculated by partner, it's tied in some way to compensation. Not us. All decisions are reached by consensus through discussion and without a vote."[11] This system motivates partners to collaborate in the service of the business and to help one another when needed. It also encourages them to take risks, because they have the support they need in the case of failure or a lean year in profits.

Flexibility and Creative Freedom

Pentagram's profit structure allows for each partner to take on the creative work that they're passionate about. For instance, Paula Scher, a Pentagram partner since 1991, has created some of her most notable work pro-bono for New York's Public Theatre.

Pentagram's non-hierarchical leadership structure also distinguishes the studio. There is no CEO or top person who runs the company. Each partner builds their own team of designers and associates who work to develop client projects, running their team much like their own small studio within the larger Pentagram ecosystem. The partners meet in person twice a year for a business retreat, during which decisions get made about, for instance, inviting a new partner into the practice.

This communal spirit is further cultivated in the offices. In Pentagram's New York space, no partner has a private office. The open space is lively, as each team works on creative projects. The partners have their own row of desks, where they may interact with one another throughout the day. As they think about building and growing as a company, this proximity and connectedness is integral to their success.

Natasha Jen joined Pentagram as a partner in April 2012. She is known for creating award-winning work for global brands such as Nike, Chanel, and Target. Her team's design work has transformed profits for companies like Van Leeuwen Ice Cream (see Chapter 1 case study). But while Jen understands the business impact of design, she says Pentagram is unique in its belief that design is not just a commodity exchanged for a price. Rather, she says, "it's a cultural entity that influences how society behaves."[12] This is central to the Pentagram ethos, and Jen says it "explains why we are reluctant to present ourselves as an agency."[13] Though Pentagram's reputation precedes it, partners often need to explain the particularities of the company to potential clients who are more familiar with the term agency and its standard operating model.

One challenge to the Pentagram business model is that each partner has to manage a business and run a team, all while trying to keep projects coming in the door. In other agency settings, these tasks might be divided among several different team members such as account executives, creative directors, and marketing managers. The pros are evident in the unique quality of work and freedom each partner has to select the jobs they choose to take and build the teams they want. Partners also get to design and be part of the process rather than serve as a figurehead to a larger creative output carried out by employees. In the end, Jen says it's worth it, because "we are able to remain relevant and still produce desirable outcomes to different clients in different sectors while being ourselves."[14] Pentagram's unique structure affords the creative freedom that she values.

Nurturing Creative Talent

Unlike many agency structures, Pentagram is not a highly tiered organization. This is significant not only in terms of partner relations and creative freedom but also because of what it means for the company's employees more broadly. For example, while most agencies have an account management team that assists in client relations, Pentagram does not believe in this structure. "Although account managers are very professional with dealing with the logistics of managing client satisfaction," Jen says of the rationale, "we feel it's important to not have a middle person and consider this a designer's job because the designer is actually producing the work."[15] But there are still roles for non-creative team members. For example, Jen's team works with a project manager to assist in scheduling and coordinating projects and meetings. For creatives, there is a very slim tier structure that includes partners with their own teams, and within a team there are associate designers and designers. Jen doesn't wait for team members to earn their way up the ladder to give them a challenging project; each person on her team has the opportunity to make a large contribution.

Jen recognizes the importance of having a great team, and she believes recruitment of top talent is a number one priority. Pentagram tends to attract top talent because of its name-brand recognition, but once they get in the door, Jen makes a point to nurture that talent and allow each team member some autonomy to develop their own creative process. Here, democratic team culture gives each member the opportunity to shine and this can motivate designers to do their best work for the team. When it comes to ego, Jen says pride in your work comes with the territory. She doesn't let it become a problem.

> My philosophy is seeing them as the best athletes possible. If you work with the best athletes, let's say Michael Jordan, you don't tell him how to play basketball, you just observe and share your observations and let them come back with their different interpretations. Give them that different feedback loop but let them know that their vision matters a lot in this conversion and this is a healthier and more productive way to handle ego.[16]

If you're not inspired by the work you do, Jen suggests figuring out the work you're truly good at and what motivates you and then focus on building more of that work. Doing work that motivates you can help you push to become better and better.

Pentagram is a unique agency model because there's not a standard hierarchy; however, there is a rigid structure, such that people can't really work across teams unless two partners choose to collaborate. As the landscape for creative work keeps evolving, it's clear there isn't a correct work style, team structure, or team size for an agency. There are many structures and roles and emerging creatives need to consider what is the best fit for them.

Marketing Agency

Definition: Marketing agencies implement and manage promotional and sales strategies to achieve a client's business goals.

Marketing agencies work on developing strategies to drive sales and entice consumers to buy a product or use a service. Smaller marketing agencies will often specialize in a given area such as social media marketing, cause-related marketing, or digital marketing, while larger marketing agencies may provide full-service marketing strategies to a wide range of clients.

OH Partners is a full-service marketing agency offering a wide range of creative capabilities including production, data analytics, strategy, and creative content. Unlike Pentagram, which doesn't have account managers serving as "middle men" between the creative team and the client, OH Partners embraces the role of account managers. In fact, throughout the creative process, the agency utilizes them to manage the relationship and communication between the client and the creative team. As with any collaboration, this working relationship between creatives and account managers can present challenges. But Brooke Harmon, OH Partners's senior director of account services, and Veda Nagpurka, the company's art director, have found working together to be an important part of the creative process. They agree that if account managers and creative professionals cultivate clear communication and strive to understand one another, they can make great work and exceed client expectations.

Interview: Brooke Harmon and Veda Nagpurka, OH Partners[17]

Brooke Harmon (Senior Director of Account Services) and Veda Nagpurka (Art Director)

Describe your role on your creative team

Harmon As a senior director of account services, I am lead on any given account. I oversee the relationship, drive strategy, manage budgets, establish processes, and resolve conflicts. I also have account management staff (like account executives) report to me that help support the day-to-day. For example, one thing that my team and I manage are internal kick-off meetings before starting a large project to allow for questions, discussion, and schedule decisions. For larger projects, the account team will set up mutual agreed upon internal check-ins—typically one mid-way and another a day or two before client review. The account team will review the work-in-progress creative to make sure it's on strategy and raise any possible red flags or issues the client could possibly bring up. Basically, my team manages all communication between the creative team and the client and we keep everyone accountable.

Nagpurka   As art director, I set the tone and provide visual direction on concepts for clients' campaigns. I also make sure that all the work that's produced on behalf of our clients is on brand and conveys the right look, tone, and feel for the brand. I collaborate with the copywriter and creative director when coming up with ideas. I also lead graphic designers and oversee the work produced by them to make sure it is accurate and up to the standards for the brand.

Our team structure is very straightforward. Our team consists of creative director, art director, copywriter, designers, production artist. I report to my creative director. For campaigns and other projects that require concepts, I collaborate with my copywriter to come up with ideas, which we then present to our creative director for approval. Currently, I have two designers on my team who I lead. A production artist helps in creating various digital or social media resizes to designing books, annual reports, or presentations and any other graphic design-related work. We have several such teams that work on specific clients. Our chief creative officer oversees all the teams.

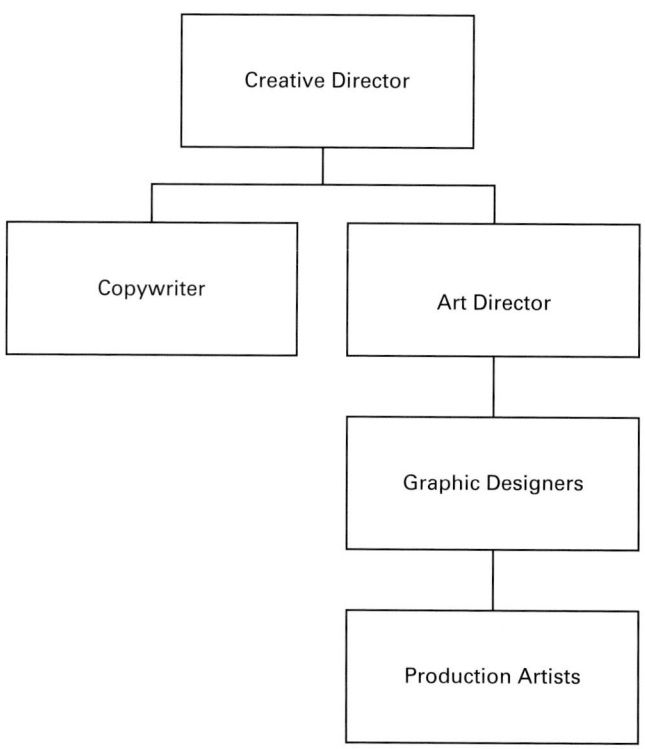

FIGURE 2.4   Team structure.
Veda Nagpurka's team structure at Oh Partners follows a traditional agency structure.

How does your team ensure that there is clear communication between all members during the creative process?

Harmon It's pretty simple. You talk often—preferably face-to-face. Project managers and project management systems are resources and tools, but they should never get in the way of communication between teams. I may overshare sometimes to creative teams, but I'd always rather err on the side of oversharing than undersharing. I gain nothing by keeping information to myself.

Nagpurka We have kick-off meetings for any new project, as well as bi-weekly status meetings to go over all the current projects and make sure they are being executed in a timely manner. During the creative process, we sometimes have internal brainstorm sessions with the team involved, depending on how big or small the project is. We also use an online project management tool where all the information about a job is documented along with due dates. Above all, if we have any questions during the process, we just walk over to each other's desks and get clarification.

What do you think makes someone an invaluable team member?

Harmon The most invaluable team members are honest, reliable, accountable, and understanding. You could have worked at the best agency on the best brands or have the most amazing creative book in town, but if teammates can't rely on you, then it doesn't matter how great you are on paper.

Nagpurka A hardworking, honest, and genuine person makes for an invaluable team member. Whether you are in a creative director role or a designer role, if you are willing to push ideas and be genuine and honest enough to make the best idea shine by putting all your hard work into the project, you are going to be successful. When you really care about the work you do, you are bound to make sure everything aligns with your team's needs and your client's needs.

What do you think makes a great leader in a creative team?

Harmon The best creative leaders I've seen empower their team to the best of their abilities. They also form unbreakable relationships with account team members. I consider the creative team leads as my counterparts and invite them to every meeting that involves strategy or creative. Great creative leaders are also empathetic, understand how to see other points of view, and are able to disagree respectfully. The best creative leaders are confident and approachable and immediately squash arrogance and out-of-control egos.

Nagpurka Someone who is not afraid to push the boundaries and think beyond the norm. Someone who trusts their team for the great work they do and encourages them to go above and beyond. Someone who sees the big picture and always keeps the team in the loop in every step of the project. Someone who is transparent and genuine makes a great leader in a creative team.

What advice would you have for an emerging creative professional who wants to work in your area of expertise?

Harmon   It takes work and you need to earn the respect of your teammates. Don't expect the relationships I've described to happen overnight—it took over twenty years of bad relationships and misguided mentorships to arrive where I am today. Mistakes happen and we *need* to learn from them to really understand and be grateful for the times that do go well.

Nagpurka   Always keep experimenting, exploring, and learning. An art director is a position best suited for someone who is an all-rounder. They are a great designer, a great story teller, amazing visualizer, someone who can ideate and think from a brand's perspective. Someone who knows the current trends on social media and knows what can emotionally connect with the consumers. Someone who has empathy. An art director should be a good collaborator as they will likely be working with a lot of people outside of their creative team such as social media, PR, media, production companies, photographers, etc. An art director should be dynamic and someone who loves their craft. Have confidence in yourself and in your creative abilities. That will take you far.

How do you cultivate relationships on a creative team?

Nagpurka   For the working relation between the creatives and account managers to be successful, it is very important that both are not only involved in all steps of the project but also have a big-picture idea of the client's expectations. It is also very important that the creatives are aware of the media plan and strategy for the given project so they can maximize the potential of their creative ideas. Gone are the days of working in a silo where each department would only be concerned about themselves. We need to learn to be collaborative interdepartmentally to create holistic campaigns and well-thought-out project executions. A successful project requires highly collaborative teamwork between media, data analysts, strategists, account managers, and creatives.

A great account manager is organized, accountable, and has excellent written and verbal communications skills. They serve as a customer service representative for the client. Account managers need to understand how creative work happens and make sure to manage client expectations for deadlines and budgets accordingly.

A great designer or art director pushes their ideas to create memorable content that fits a client's needs. A great team leader will empower their team members to make their best work. They often present client feedback to the creative team and are often mediators between the creative team and the client. This can help free up time for the creative team to come up with great creative content, rather than spending too much time in meetings and working to interpret feedback. By making sure to cultivate a team spirit rather than an "us vs. them" mentality, account managers and creative team members like Harmon and Nagpurka build a sense of trust and enjoy a collaboration that results in happy clients.

Branding Agency

Definition: A branding agency offers "research, planning, copywriting, implementation, and stewardship, all of which are necessary to make decisions about how a brand unfolds over time and not just what it looks like."[18]

Branding agencies create and develop brand strategies for clients. Brand agency teams spend a lot of time understanding a brand through research and data. For instance, before delving into a new project, the team may interview the client, their employees, and their customers to uncover the brand's current message and check if it aligns with the client's goals. A brand is not a logo, but the sum of all the impressions that an organization creates. A brand is how an organization is perceived, and without a clear brand strategy, organizations struggle to communicate their message to their intended audience. That's where companies like Principle come in.

Like most branding agencies, Principle examines brand strategy, brand identity, and brand standards based on a company's purpose and values. They focus on the big picture. The output can take many forms. Working for a brand agency might involve developing (or redesigning) a logo and visual style of a brand. It can focus on digital media, naming, written content, printed material, or all of the above. As Principle describes on their website, they strive to "spark an emotional connection with people waiting to embrace your brand."[19] This emotional connection helps organizations build meaningful relationships with their audience and differentiate from other, similar brands.

Flexibility for Growth

Despite modeling her branding agency after Pentagram, Allyson Lack structured her business a bit differently. When the company was founded, Principle operated as a single agency that offered an experienced team providing multifaceted branding services. However, each of the three partners ran their own independent LLC and essentially hired one another to collaborate as a team. This worked well because it was easy to set up; each team member could manage their end of the business independently, and each team member was operating in a different US state with different business license requirements. This is very different from Pentagram, where each partner owns an equal share in the business. Lack attributes this difference to the more established success of Pentagram: "The difference between Pentagram and Principle is Pentagram is comprised of people who have already made it and are going to the next level. We didn't have that kind of weight. We were fledgling, fearless, and hungry; for us it was sink or swim."[20]

Principle's model offered each of the three founding partners total personal freedom. When one partner wanted to leave to pursue a career path in user experience design, it was easy, because she could dissolve her LLC without affecting the others'. She could move on from the business without the other partners having to buy her out. Principle's structure has changed since it was founded in 2005 and it is now run exclusively by Allyson Lack. It may evolve again in the future, but what is consistent is that Principle still offers branding services for clients.

Advertising Agency

Definition: Advertising agencies create, plan, and implement paid ad spots and sometimes other forms of promotion for their clients.

While branding is about the vision and mission of a company, advertising focuses on how an organization or brand communicates these values to its customers and audience. Clients usually hire advertising agencies to develop a campaign that focuses on delivering a clear message.

Creative professional Tom Drymalski was the executive creative director at Publicis, one of the top five biggest advertising agencies in the world, when he led his team to develop the Citi Bike campaign sponsored by Citibank. This case study showcases how a large creative team works to develop a multifaceted brand and advertising campaign.

CASE STUDY: CITI BIKE: COLLABORATING ON A MULTIFACETED CAMPAIGN

Creative collaboration often involves many players from different organizations. This case study looks at a multifaceted campaign to explore a large agency process.

Project
Citi Bike "Unlock New York" campaign

Client
Citibank

Creative Team
Agency: Publicis
Project lead: Tom Drymalski

Duration
2013

Description
Tom Drymalski's team had the chance to create some of their most visible branding when they were assigned to a multidisciplinary project for Citibank. Citibank had signed on to become the sole sponsor of New York City's bike-sharing program, and Publicis was the agency hired to assist in getting this program branded and rolled out to the public. As part of one of the largest ad agencies in the world, the NYC Publicis office was able to take on account and strategy, creative, and digital development for this project. The Publicis teams collaborated closely with both their client, Citibank and the bike share owner, Alta. The project was overseen by a creative leadership team that included Drymalski and several other executive level team members who worked together to shape the project from multiple angles including strategy, creative, and digital.

As a leader on the creative team, Drymalski's group was tasked with the branding and promotion aspect of this highly collaborative project. In his own words, "our job was to generate excitement and brand the whole program."[21]

When Drymalski's team was first shown the bikes, they were bright green with a small back panel where the team was told to place the Citi Bike logo. The creative team suggested redesigning the entire bike, branding it by replacing the green with Citibank blue. Their goal was to make a bigger impact for the client and the program while also adding functionality.

Process
Drymalski's team launched a campaign called "Unlock New York," infusing a unique look and feel into posters and print ads as well as the docking stations and the bikes themselves. With the assistance of the digital team, they added to the program's functionality by creating a smartphone app that helps riders find bikes and plan routes to explore the city.

The campaign became so big that they had to bring on more teams to help realize their vision. Drymalski, who served as the project's executive creative director, describes the many moving parts: "We had two creative teams developing concepts for the advertising, a full digital team focused on user experience design, two other creative directors, and an account team."[22] The client was also a big part of the team because they were willing to take the risk to develop this huge campaign, and it paid off in media coverage, brand recognition, and goodwill from residents and tourists who use the bike share program. In fact, Citi Bike became so linked to the Citibank brand that bike share customers started going to bank locations to try and get a flat tire fixed!

Outcome

The Citi Bike program garnered high visibility such as front-page headlines in the media, a spot on *The Late Show*, and even made the cover of *The New Yorker* magazine. In the first six hours of going live, Citi Bike signed up more than 16,000 members. The campaign was also the winner of Best in Show at the 2014 Financial Communications Society Portfolio Awards.

FIGURE 2.5 Citi Bike docking station.
Citi Bike bikes parked at a NYC docking station.

FIGURE 2.6 *The New Yorker* magazine.

The Citi Bike campaign was so successful in its reach and visibility that it gained wide media coverage, including the cover of *The New Yorker* magazine.

FIGURE 2.7 Mobile app.

The Citi Bike mobile app wasn't part of the original scope of the Citi Bike project, but this functionality is at the heart of the program's success, earning numerous awards including a 2014 Webby Award.

FIGURE 2.8 "Unlock New York."

The Citi Bike campaign slogan was titled "Unlock New York" and was visible throughout the city to engage residents and tourists alike in taking advantage of the benefits that a Citi Bike has to offer.

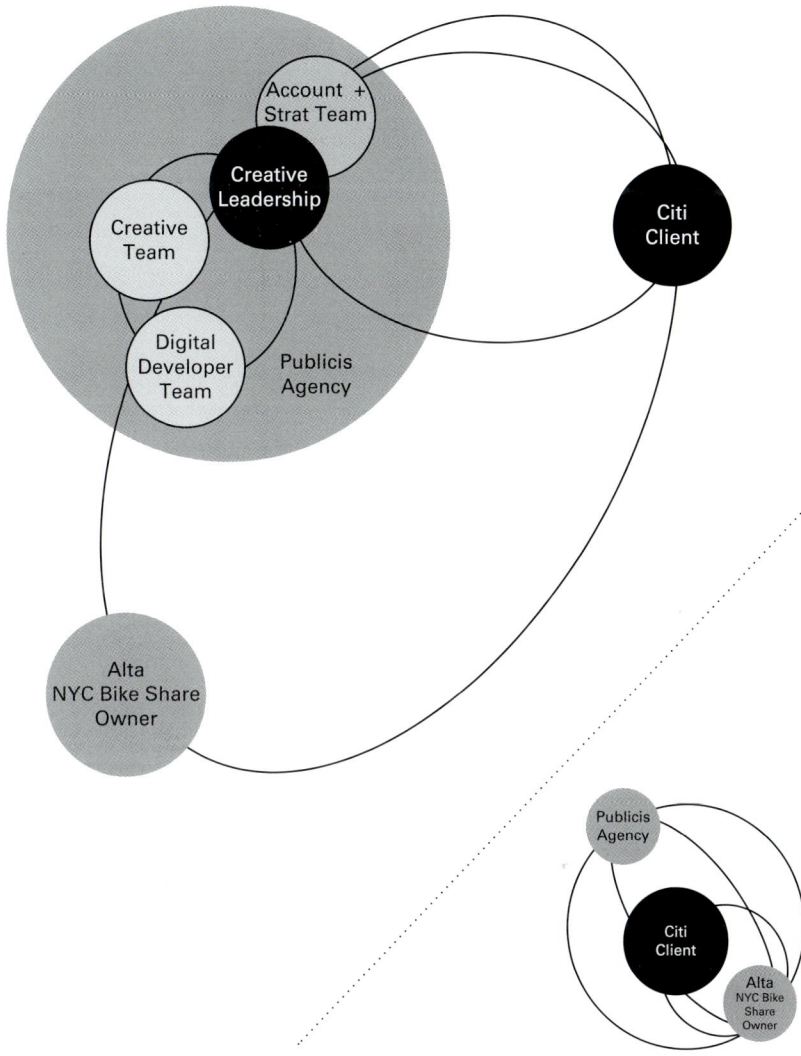

FIGURE 2.9 Citi Bike project—team structure.

This project depended on collaboration between teams both within Publicis and with other stakeholders, including Citi, the sole sponsor of the bike share program, and Alta, the bike share owner. The success of the project is intertwined with the strength of the creative teams.

Questions for Thought

What about this agency type makes this project possible?

How would the process look different if the project had been carried out by a small branding agency?

Consider a creative project you're working on now. How might you push boundaries and think big to reimagine the project?

Consultancy

Definition: "A consultancy is a group that advises and coaches on design strategy and direction in a way that addresses the whole client or company, rather than focusing on a specific marketing, advertising, or product need that can be answered through a deliverable. The visuals that it produces are usually handed off for final execution to in-house design groups or external production studios."[23]

Working for a creative consultancy means getting involved in the deeper aspects of an organization to uncover its true value. It requires a creative specialty such as design or copywriting, but it also requires excellent people skills and empathy. To help a company find its authentic brand voice involves asking great questions and, most importantly, listening carefully. It sometimes requires acting as a mediator by asking tough questions of the team and working through challenges that might be beyond the scope of the creative brief. It can also mean acting as cheer leader and supporter by nurturing a client's vision to help them define it in a more tangible way. Intangible communication skills are invaluable for this. Learning to understand other people and their unique points of view helps a creative professional develop important skills, and looking beyond one's own experiences and biases is valuable in any professional setting.

It can be challenging for companies to develop a clear brand voice and identity. Braid Creative is an example of consultancy that works with clients to help them with their voice to get to the heart of what they want to say and create a vision for where they're going. It works to give clients a renewed focus and confidence to share what they do with potential and existing customers. Braid Creative is known for its unique method, with tools and techniques to help its clients understand and define their unique value. Like a branding agency, it provides strategy, design, and copywriting services. But what distinguishes it as a consultancy is its holistic approach, which involves coaching, strategy, and brand visioning with its clients. Through its distinct process called The Braid Method™, the Braid creative team works alongside its clients and ensures they are collaborating in the creative process together.

When starting their company, Braid Creative founders Tara Street and Kathleen Shannon began with a clarity of purpose. Shannon knew that if she were to run her own agency, she wanted to be 100 percent who she was. Street understood that while maintaining a sustainable business and paying the bills are important goals, that is not a purpose. Her purpose was to own her creative expertise and convey that knowledge and experience to instill confidence in her clients. As Street and Shannon conceived a brand vision for their own entrepreneurial endeavor, they realized they were developing a method that could help other creative entrepreneurs find their voice.[24] Their creative collaboration with one another became the foundation for how Street and Shannon collaborated with clients.

Production Company

Definition: "A production company offers production services to both studios and agencies, usually for motion graphics or large-scale digital products."[25]

The term "production company" often calls to mind large movie studios that make big blockbuster hits. While these are production companies, not all production companies look like this. Production companies can work in new media, film, video games, interactive media, and more, and they produce creative work for clients, much like an advertising or branding agency. They handle the production of content, often in the form of motion-based media such as commercials and social media ads. Some larger agencies might have a production team on-site, while others hire out. Due to increasing demand for video content, there are also some production companies that cut out the agency and go straight to client to assist with creative production needs.

Table of Content, cofounded by Tom Drymalski in 2018, after he left Publicis, is one such company. Designed to meet the high demand of motion-based media content and the quick turnaround expected by twenty-first-century consumers, this production company works with brands to tell their stories. With the staggering amount of smartphone users and wide availability of high-speed internet, video streaming is increasing for the average consumer and brands large and small are hustling to keep up by telling their stories through unique and engaging motion media content such as animation, video, and live streaming. While Table of Content has been deliberately structured to offer a broad spectrum of capabilities including communications planning, social media strategy, creative development, branding, design, editorial, and production, there are other types of production companies that are more specialized.

Motion Graphics Studio

Definition: A motion graphics studio creates video marketing strategies for clients utilizing creative motion and animation techniques.

Falling under the production company umbrella, a motion graphics studio offers a more focused type of video marketing strategies for clients. Typically, this involves short-form motion-based work that features creative motion and animation techniques. In many cases, a motion graphics studio has a unique specialty, such as creating kinetic type within projects. This work can utilize 2D or 3D animation technology and may be created for marketing, advertising, or other creative promotional material. For example, Greenhaus GFX, founded by Helen Greene, specializes in creating film title sequences. (A title sequence is a short motion graphics piece that appears at the beginning of a film to set the tone and introduce the film.) Film studios hire Greenhaus GFX to produce the title sequence, which is, in essence, a promotional tool that helps generate excitement among the audience for the feature-length event.

Leading and Learning

In her role as leader, Greene relies on producers to make her company's operations run smoothly. Working much like account managers in advertising agencies, producers manage budgets and timelines, book freelancers, and oversee projects to make sure teams are working effectively and efficiently. Greene has worked with some producers who enter the field with a business or communication background, but she finds the most success with producers who have training in art and motion design. This experience allows a producer to more fully understand the timing and work required to complete a complex motion project. And, if the need arises, they can jump in and do some of the work themselves. Greene stays up-to-date on new technology and techniques so that she, too, can jump in on a project when necessary. If she needs to, she can get into the programs and work on a title sequence, but perhaps more importantly she can communicate more clearly when something isn't working. Her advice to emerging creatives is to always keep learning. "By staying up-to-date," she says, "I can understand when the camera work is wrong or why the extrusions don't look correct and I can give clear feedback using the proper terms."[26]

Animation Studio

Definition: Animation studios are entertainment companies that use similar tools as motion graphics studios but typically in the service of narrative series or film.

While the technical process for creating motion graphics is the same as creating animation, animation studios vary quite a bit in their structure from motion graphics studios. This has to do primarily with the type of work created by each. Creative production companies and motion graphics studios focus on brand promotion via short-form motion pieces such as commercials or social media content, while animation studios are entertainment companies that typically create longer-form, narrative-based series or films. A 3D animation studio works in a production pipeline where once an idea and storyboard are developed, the production team works on layout, modeling, texture, rigging, animation, special effects, lighting, and rendering. They conclude with post-production to finalize the film before making it available to audiences. While many people confuse motion graphics and animation studios, the animation pipeline is a unique creative process that differs from the creative agency models discussed in this chapter because instead of working for various clients, the animation studio focuses on the creation of one larger project: a film or narrative series.

Filmmaker, educator, and author of the book *Animated Storytelling,* Liz Blazer points out that animation studios such as Pixar or Dreamworks require many specialized positions to complete a feature-length animation. "There are so many positions in animation," Blazer says. "You can be a rigger, texturer, or an animator who just does the movement, but in motion graphics you have to be a generalist because the teams are smaller."[27] As an animator you can spend your entire career on smaller parts of the whole. Blazer describes one such instance: "I have a friend who did lip design their whole career and just worked on the way that lips moved to make a character talk."[28] While it's a bit different than the other agency structures mentioned here, animation studios require much of the same collaborative skills.

Depending on an agency's size, structure, and type, a given technical creative skill can be put to many different uses and translate to many career paths. When reflecting on your professional path, consider not only your technical skills but also your creativity, soft skills, and professional goals.

State of the Agency World

The traditional art director/copywriter team is perhaps the oldest example of a creative team, yet it is the most threatened due to the wide range of changes happening in technology and communication. The rapid changes in media and communication require teams that have additional expertise, because just an art director and copywriter is not effective in every creative challenge. Agencies and studios are adapting as the creative world continues to accelerate further into the twenty-first century. Successful agencies are moving away from a one-size-fits-all approach and towards more flexible team structures to accommodate the needs of individual projects. They also have created more fluid team structures that shift and offer more interdisciplinary skill sets, depending on the project. Many creative agencies no longer rely on billing clients on annual retainers, where income is guaranteed for a full year. Instead, they must create great work on short-term projects to keep the client coming back for more. While this can seem like a negative forecast for agencies, it is, in fact, an opportunity for them to evolve.

How Agencies Evolve

The benefits of creative work are becoming so widely celebrated that many organizations are no longer hiring agencies to do their creative work but instead launching in-house teams (the subject of Chapter 3) to bring creative under one unified vision, to streamline creative work, and to improve profits. This is changing the way agencies operate. For instance, when one of Greenhaus GFX's regular clients decided to move their operations in-house and build their own motion graphics department, Helen Greene had to rethink her team structure. She now operates with a leaner team and brings in freelance professionals as projects demand. As the field continues to evolve, Greene may need to pivot yet again, but she's confident she'll be ready.[29] She is but one of many in the agency world who have seen these types of shifts across creative industries.

Rapid changes in technology are another issue for creative agencies. Some may find this a challenge, while others see opportunity in working with new creative technologies. Groove Jones is an example of a creative technology company that has earned a reputation as a leader in augmented reality, virtual reality, machine learning, and artificial intelligence application development. To keep up with the latest changes, Groove Jones teams live in the world of "beta" and are always evolving with the newest developments in creative technologies. This is how the company stays relevant in the fast-paced world of technological innovation. But it's not easy. Teams are constantly striving to narrow the gap between creative design and technology, always looking for ways to empower artists to realize their visions. For instance, to commemorate NBA player Dirk Nowitzki's retirement on April 9, 2019, Groove Jones built four augmented reality experiences including a 68ft x 193ft wall mural with augmented reality activation. Located just blocks from where Nowitzki's team, the Dallas Mavericks, play, fans were instructed to point their phones at the artwork in order to see Nowitzki come to life and take twenty-one shots for each of his twenty-one seasons with the team. Fans who attended the game on April 9 also enjoyed augmented reality experiences on a commemorative game ticket, a commemorative poster, and a game clapper.[30]

With its innovative platforms and experiences, Groove Jones is well positioned to influence the creative technologies of the future. The company has some predictions about the future of creative technology, including more advanced graphics, with the development of faster graphics processors allowing for shifts like real-time raytracing technology. Founder Dan Ferguson envisions big changes in user interaction: "I see the paradigms of UI and user interaction changing significantly as we move more to hand and eye recognition and eventually full body recognition."[31] This type of foreshadowing is what keeps the company evolving. Always open to and imagining new possibilities, Groove Jones keeps pushing boundaries of user experience.

While some agencies have held fast to their business models—Pentagram's, for instance, has hardly changed since it opened in 1972—others are constantly evolving. Pentagram partner Natasha Jen points to R/GA as a model of radical transformation in the agency world: "R/GA has an interesting business model that has evolved three or four times in the decades since Pentagram was founded."[32]

The company started out creating movie titles, and then evolved into an internet business agency. Now it takes on all aspects of communication and business design. It even has a team that focuses exclusively on venture capitalism. While both companies are extremely successful creative agencies, they provide a compelling contrast to one another. While R/GA has adapted on a large scale over the years, changing its offerings to meet client needs, Pentagram has maintained its founding principles and structure, asserting its relevance by inviting new partners to the team who bring new capabilities and a fresh perspective to the business.

Right now, many companies are transitioning to the organic "pod" team structures as the old "bloated" agency model increasingly proves itself unsustainable. Leeann Leahy, CEO of the VIA Agency, restructured based on this concept, stating, "One solution to eliminate waste and flatten the organization is to restructure into a multi-discipline pod system."[33]

Teams that want to succeed must evolve. Sometimes, this requires rethinking entire team structures. But based on the project at hand, the work can help define the needs of the team. There's no perfect formula for success and this is what is most daunting of all. As the technology keeps speeding forward and new business models interrupt the old ones, creative teams must keep pace to get messages seen and heard.

EXERCISE: INTERVIEW OUTSIDE YOUR SCOPE

This chapter used a series of examples to introduce you to a number of different types of creative agencies. In this exercise, you'll dig deeper into creative agencies by interviewing a design professional to learn more about the agency they work for and their experience there.

Consider yourself an investigative reporter for your career and get ready to interview a creative professional from your own community. Start by doing research on agencies in your local area. Which catch your eye as most interesting? Find someone from your favorite agency and reach out to ask if they have time to tell you a little about their job and agency over coffee. Be sure to ask about the local design scene . . . you might find a whole community of like-minded creatives in your own region!

Step 1: Research Local Agencies
How many creative agencies can you find within 10, 20, and 50 miles of where you live? Try to find at least five and dig deeper. What are their

creative specialties? What is their mission statement? What do they value? How big are their teams? Who are their clients? What kind of projects do they work on? Can you envision yourself working at any of these agencies?

Research Tip: When searching online, try using all the different agency types mentioned in this chapter because, as you now know, an agency might describe itself as an advertising agency, a consultancy, a design studio, etc. Also, look to your local professional organizations for affiliate agencies or sponsors.

Step 2: Pick One Agency to Focus On

Based on your research, pick one of the agencies from your list. Try to find a specific person you can reach out to, such as an art director or other creative role you're interested in learning more about. If you can't find a specific name, try the agency's general email and send a polite inquiry for an informational interview.

Here's a letter template you can adapt for your own use:

Subject line: Informational Interview Request
Dear [first name],
I'm an aspiring [graphic designer/copywriter/user experience designer/etc.] and a huge fan of [company's creative work]. I'm writing to ask if I could [take you out for a coffee/set up a Zoom call/other means of interview delivery] and conduct an informational interview to learn more about [your chosen creative industry].

Thank you so much for your time, I look forward to hearing from you.

Regards,
[your full name]
[contact info in email signature]

Once you've found someone to interview, make it clear you're interested in learning more about their work, but keep it casual—this isn't a job interview! Schedule a time to meet, make sure you clarify how much time the person is able to spend with you, and offer to buy your interviewee a coffee or lunch as a way to thank them for their time.

Step 3: Plan for the Interview

Once you've secured an interview, it helps to plan some questions in advance.
This is an informational interview, so ask questions about their day-to-day work, schedule, client communication, team structure, and creative process. If time is limited, don't try to cram it all into one session.

Step 4: Conduct the Interview

Now that you've scheduled and planned, it's time to conduct the interview. First and foremost, make sure you arrive on time! You don't have to dress in formal attire, but consider business casual style dress. While it's helpful to be prepared, don't feel like you have to get to every question on your list. Use your questions to get the conversation started, and then see how it progresses from there. Make sure to respect your interviewee's time and wrap up at the agreed time.

Step 5: Reflection

Within 24 hours of conducting your interview, write down your impressions of the person you talked to. What did you learn that you can apply to your own goals for working on a creative team? Did they offer any helpful advice?

Don't forget to write a short thank-you follow-up for their time and in the future, consider giving back to your creative community through future mentorship opportunities.

3 IN-HOUSE TEAMS

Daniel McLemore worked on a wide range of creative teams before becoming a leader on an in-house creative team. McLemore's first job out of college was a full-time position creating commercials and promotional graphics for a local television station. To meet client needs, he had to pick up new skills such as creating graphics and writing scripts. By the time he landed his next major creative job at an advertising agency, he had developed a wide range of skills and continued to build more. His experience included meeting with clients, doing graphic design, writing scripts for commercials, and going on film shoots. Having worn many different hats at his television station and ad agency jobs, he was well positioned to be the one-stop shop for all things design when he took his next job at his alma mater, Lamar University.

It didn't take long for McLemore to learn that working on an in-house creative team was a lot different than working on an agency team. While his creative skills were still the same, he found the way he applied them was different. Because he was only working on the development of one brand, the work was much more focused. He could make long-term plans and see them through over a period of years, whereas at an agency, a long term project typically lasts only several months at most. With that time and focus, McLemore was able to showcase how creative work added value to the institution, increasing enrollment and brand awareness. With a long-term vision, he was able to help grow the in-house creative team and work towards new goals year after year.[1]

As McLemore's experience shows, in-house creative teams add value to an organization by offering deep knowledge of the company's needs and practices. While an agency needs to research every client, an in-house team is already intimately familiar with its company's priorities, challenges, and goals. This built-in knowledge can help shape creative strategy.

The Value of In-house Creative Teams

Bringing creative work in-house can add great value to an organization. While "in-house" refers to the internal creative staff working directly for an organization, "client side" refers to focused work on one brand (in contrast to the "agency side" of creative work, which involves working for an agency). In an agency, an organization would have been referred to as a client, but now they are part of the same team. For the sake of clarity in this chapter, the term in-house will be used to describe creative teams that support a brand from within the organization.

There is a growing trend to bring more work in-house. According to recent industry reports, in-house creative teams are experiencing growth, and team members report high job satisfaction working in-house. These reports also suggest that qualified talent is hard to come by.[2] As growth in the agency world has slowed, there is great opportunity for skilled creatives to jump onto in-house teams and make waves from within.[3]

Though there are many opportunities for in-house creatives, there are also challenges. One of the biggest is being misunderstood and undervalued by the other arms of the company. Many company executives and clients view in-house creative teams as service providers and mistake their job as "making things look pretty." According to one report, 60 percent of creative leaders state that "gaining respect from internal clients or value recognition is one of their greatest challenges."[4] In order to combat this obstacle, in-house creatives must often educate and collaborate with others to showcase how creative work can achieve high-level business goals such as earning more profit and capturing more impressions from potential consumers. Ultimately, it's a matter of qualifying and quantifying value to make it understandable so that other departments within the organization can grasp a creative team's full potential to impact the organization.

Emma Sexton understands the value design can bring business. Since 2013, her UK-based consultancy has provided value to businesses by offering design services to clients. Not a typical agency model, Sexton's company serves as a "plug and play" in-house team for companies that don't have their own in-house offering. As Sexton puts it, "I wanted to help solve a problem where businesses either don't understand how design is adding value to their business, or what the opportunities are."[5] Rather than start another agency, Sexton instead decided to launch a company dedicated to amplifying the business impact of design. Her team of designers are familiar with one another and can serve as the in-house team for an organization until their creative needs are met, or until they're ready to build out a full creative team of their own. They have skills in both design and business and can hit the ground running.

Sexton also consults for in-house creative teams. In this role, she seeks to transform in-house creatives from mere service providers on a "detached island of creative" into creative collaborators who work alongside executives to develop creative business strategy.⁶ She observed that creatives often don't know how to articulate the impact of their work, resulting in members of an organization outside the creative team not knowing what they do, why they do it, or how it matters. Sexton's company works to demystify the creative process for business leaders and assist creatives in showcasing their value.

Sexton's "plug and play" model is atypical for in-house teams. Most in-house creative teams consist of full-time employees working internally for an organization. They can add value because their strong connection to the brand and access to internal resources augments their ability to respond to organizational needs quickly and efficiently. For example, during one month in the spring of 2018, the Spotify in-house creative team developed a full underground takeover of New York City's Broadway-Lafayette subway station. The immersive experience included wall-size art, music codes, downloadable playlists, a unique hashtag, and even specially designed tickets to round out the experience for visitors.⁷ The tight timeline was only manageable because the campaign was created by an in-house team already familiar with the company. As Spotify's then vice-president of brand and creative, Jackie Jantos explained, "That opportunity presented itself and four weeks later that execution was live. There are very few partners who can work in that way."⁸ Though the effort itself yielded no profit, its visibility and branding were transformative in that they produced public goodwill.

In-house/Agency Collaboration

In-house creative teams come in a wide range of sizes, structures, and capabilities, and sometimes they need to hire outside creative help to fulfill client goals. For instance, a small in-house team might need to hire a production company to create video production work. Without a full-time member with the needed skill set, it's beneficial to outsource rather than stretch the team thin by asking them to acquire new skills for a single project.

It can be tricky to develop a strong collaboration between in-house team members and contract workers. Tension can arise when the in-house team's sense of brand ownership and connection becomes territorial, or the contractors fail to build trust or open communication with the in-house team.

Beverly Bethge and William Faust, senior partners at the Ohio-based creative consultancy Ologie, have examined how in-house teams and agencies work together and offer solutions for how to make this relationship deliver the best possible outcomes. "It's one thing for in-house creative teams and outside agencies to collaborate," they write. "It's another for them to form truly integrated teams."⁹ To integrate, they recommend creating a "living creative brief" that provides flexibility on both sides while the creative process is underway. This allows for changes that may build stronger results in the final product. Whenever possible, it helps to consider having teams work together, even if only part-time or remotely.

This can enable teams to get on the same page and to share and reflect on their respective expertise and ideas, as well as both take ownership of the project.

They also recommend putting together a team with an equal number of in-house and agency members to create balance and facilitate a safe and open space for critique and evaluation. Additionally, shared collaborative spaces can activate creativity and ideas, especially for pinning work as the project progresses to allow more stakeholders within the organization to buy into the newly developed creative plans. Sharing knowledge between in-house and agency teams is also a great way to break the ice and build trust. By having experts from each side present a new skill or lead a break-out session, the two sides of the team can learn and grow together. Finally, Bethge and Faust suggest teams celebrate the work they created together, either through informal gatherings or by submitting to award competitions as a collective group. Mobilizing these strategies, in-house teams can optimize their working relationship with contracted agency teams.

CASE STUDY: INSIDE OUT AWARDS: CELEBRATING IN-HOUSE CREATIVE WORK

Creative projects don't always begin with a client brief. In this case study, a passion project becomes a highly collaborative annual industry event.

Project
Inside Out Awards

Client
This is not a client project, but instead a community-driven project developed to support and celebrate in-house design teams.

Creative Team
Emma Sexton, Found & CEO, Hands Down! Agency

Duration
Founded in 2013 as the In-House Design Awards and ongoing.

Description
The Inside Out Awards were founded and developed by Emma Sexton, founder and CEO of Hands Down! Agency. With support from her team, sponsors, and in-house collaborators, the event has grown year after year since 2013.

Sexton, who is also an in-house design consultant, founded the awards to help in-house creative teams earn credibility in their field and combat the perception that in-house creative work is not as innovative as agency work. The In-House Design Awards respond to the unique work of in-house teams by focusing on criteria that are specific to the creative demands and collaborations that happen within in-house teams. As Sexton explains, "Traditionally, the majority of design awards have focused purely on the creative execution of projects, but when I worked in-house I always found it difficult to find award categories for the projects and impact our team had delivered."[10] Traditional design and advertising awards celebrate creative excellence and tend to recognize the high-visibility projects in which agencies specialize. As a result, in-house projects that appear modest but have big business impact often get overlooked.

Process

While in-house teams can submit to traditional award competitions, the Inside Out Awards celebrate and reward creative work that is specific to the challenges and opportunities faced by an in-house creative team. Unique categories for judgment include specific in-house areas such as "Best Example of Collaboration with an Outside Agency"; "Best Example

FIGURE 3.1 Emma Sexton at the Inside Out Awards 2019.

As the founder of the Inside Out Awards, Emma Sexton has helped raise the visibility of in-house creative work in the UK.

of Internal Collaboration," honoring creative collaboration and partnership with other divisions of an organization; "Best Internal Rebrand," recognizing in-house work to transform an organization's image; and "Impact on the Overall Business," celebrating measurable improvements in-house teams have on business outcomes, including profits and brand visibility.

Every year the number of entries increases, and a growing community of in-house teams has rallied around the event as it adds credibility and value to the work they're doing. The awards help to boost team morale and build connections among in-house creatives.

Outcome

Award winners have observed that recognition can be an important step in transforming an in-house creative team. as previous winner, the NSPCC, discovered. "Winning an award gave our team a massive boost," explains Sue Hornsby, creative director of the National Society for the Prevention of Child Cruelty (UK). "Not only was it great to get recognition for a project that we were really proud to have worked on, but it also helped us to forge stronger relationships with other people and teams at the NSPCC." After her team won, they saw "more and more people picking us as the first choice to take on projects," allowing them to "take on more exciting challenges as a team and make more of a difference to the organization."[11]

Pentland Brands was the Inside Out Awards 2019 "Best Project" winner for the "Be Part of It" campaign. Pentland is a family of sports, outdoor, and lifestyle brands, including the rugby brand, Canterbury. This was Canterbury's biggest global brand campaign to date, and "it brought to life the inclusivity and togetherness of the rugby community in the build-up to the recent Rugby World Cup in Japan."[12] The in-house creative team was tasked with the strategy and development of the campaign. James Benn, senior art director said of the in-house teamwork, "Great work happens when there's mutual respect and trust between all involved. It's been a huge team effort and [winning an industry award] a great way to top off a complex 13-month cross-functional collaboration."[13] Like any creative team, building trust and comradery on an in-house team is essential to making great work.

Questions for Thought

What kind of achievements have been meaningful in your life? What do you aspire to achieve in the future?

FIGURE 3.2 The 2019 Best Project Award winners from Pentland Brands.

The 2019 Inside Out Best Project Award went to Pentland Brands: Canterbury "Be Part of It" Rugby World Cup campaign. This was Canterbury's largest-ever global campaign and the team collaborated with many internal and external partners to pull it off.

Does the award recognition change your perception of the "Be Part of It" campaign?

How do your favorite brands develop creative work? Try to find out if it's through agency or in-house teams.

FIGURE 3.3 "Be Part of It" campaign graphics.

The theme of the "Be Part of It" campaign was to promote inclusivity and togetherness in the rugby community, and this was achieved through a campaign representing the diverse cultures in rugby as well as the team spirit and camaraderie among players and fans.

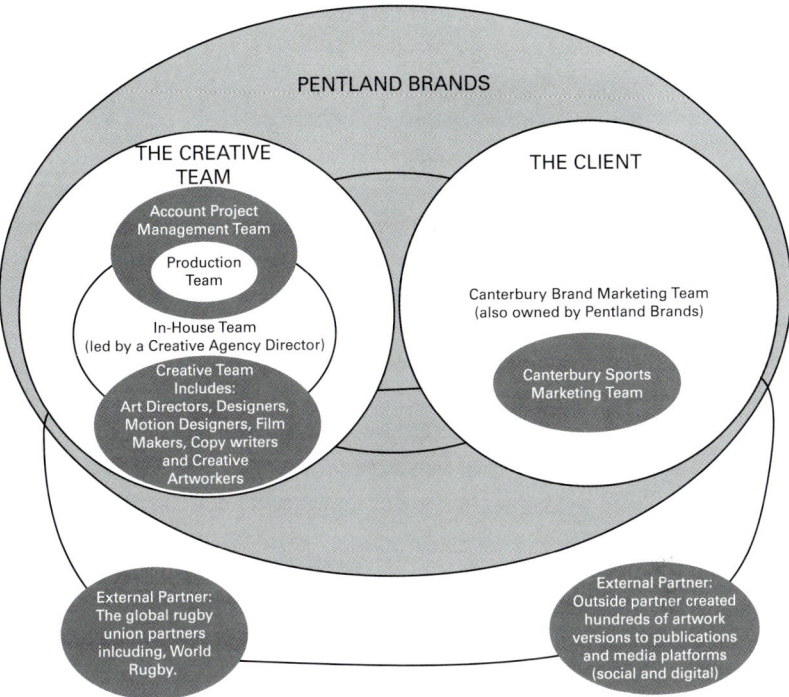

FIGURE 3.4 Canterbury "Be Part of It" team stucture.

The "Be Part of It" campaign showcases how in-house creative teams are often structured the same as agency teams, and, for large projects such as this, these internal teams must collaborate much like an agency–client relationship. In this case, the Canterbury creative team worked with the Canterbury marketing team as their client, and they also worked with external partners from the global rugby union and various media platforms.

Working In-house Towards a Common Goal

One defining feature of in-house creative work is the structure of the relationship between creative professionals and clients. In-house creative departments at small organizations are frequently integrated into the day-to-day workflow. By contrast, some in-house teams at larger companies function similarly to a traditional agency where the team is separated from the organization and creative work is "requested" and billed, much like you would see in any advertising agency; agencies generally bill clients on an hourly basis, but some agencies work on retainers or use project-based rates. (Despite this separation, the "clients" and creatives still work for the same organization and share many common goals.) There are three reasons for this type of structure. First, it's a familiar model with a strong track record in the agency world. Second, when time is tracked, an organization can more easily measure costs and outcomes; many in-house agencies are developed as a cost-saving measure, so these types of metrics become valuable in justifying expenses and hiring more team members. Third, brands can track their own data more efficiently and make more informed decisions about media buying as they develop strategies for creative campaigns and decide where to promote their brand. This explains the advantages of in-house for companies. But what does it mean for the creatives who work for them?

In-house work often suffers from a poor reputation. Some perceive stagnancy in the long-term focus on a single brand. Yet committing to a single organization offers an opportunity to see development as ideas grow and transform over time. For instance, Daniel McLemore has helped shape a cohesive brand identity that unifies the Lamar University campus, allows for a consistent vision across all communication channels, and establishes a locally, nationally, and globally recognizable brand. Since 2014 when he started at Lamar, McLemore has seen the in-house marketing and creative team grow from just five roles to over twenty, with more to come. The marketing team defines and implements brand standards and collaborates with colleagues across campus to develop materials to assist in recruiting new students, promoting events, and spreading the word about faculty, staff, and student accomplishments and innovation.

Agency work is much different in that the standards aren't usually directed by the creative team. As McLemore explains, "Working in-house, the creative team is directing what's being done. In an agency, if the client doesn't like the work, nine times out of ten the client is going to win and they're going to get whatever they want done because the agency has to keep the door open and they have to get paid."[14] Not only do in-house teams have more authority to defend their work, they can also launch branding initiatives themselves. For instance, McLemore's team developed a brand ambassador program by leveraging students on campus to help investigate brand awareness and help spread the university message. It would be rare for an agency to have the opportunity to independently instigate such a program, or work with students for as long as McLemore's team did.

Projects like these require extensive coordination. To lead his team effectively, McLemore must coordinate with his entire team. Describing a typical meeting with his creative team colleagues, he explains, "I meet with the social media manager, the graphic designer, and the video specialist, and we all discuss various projects that we all are working on together, but my job is to ask, 'what do you need?' and coordinating the project to make sure they reach a successful outcome."[15] For McLemore, successful leadership involves providing resources for his team.

Different Kinds of In-house Work

Designer Angelica McKinley works at the intersection of technology, news, and media, and has used her expertise to contribute to in-house creative teams with very different priorities. At the *New York Times*, McKinley worked on digital products without considering longevity, because it's not practical for the media hub to maintain the code and update years of backlogged content. "It's kind of like temporary digital artwork," she explains. "It's meant to live for this period of time."[16] One such "artwork" was McKinley's design for the article "Harriet Tubman's Path to Freedom," which included embedded text, photos, an interactive map, and video content that update with the reader as they scroll through the narrative.[17] Rather than regularly revising the piece to reflect the newest technological tools, the design, which was recognized with an Award of Excellence from the Society of News Design in 2018, will remain an artifact of its making in 2017. Just as old news articles are not revised when new information emerges, neither will McKinley's design be modified. New tools will be used for new articles, whereas old capabilities will remain part of the historical record.

By contrast, in her role as one of the founding members of Slack's web team for brand, McKinley had to innovate new ways to entice visitors to adopt the Slack platform for their teams. Unlike the *New York Times*, with its well-established brand, Slack was a young company still figuring out how to communicate the brand and build design processes. Building these design processes to create consistency of communication and clarity for new customers was an essential first step to establishing a strong brand presence.

On this team, McKinley led the implementation for the redesigned Slack.com and created a modular system to speed up the construction of landing pages and new components. Additionally, using her experience working within the *New York Times*'s well-defined design system, McKinley redesigned her team's infrastructure by building new processes and best practices. Although less quantifiable, this work included "creating design strategy brainstorming sessions to better define creative briefs; working with external vendors for sourcing freelance designers, purchasing typefaces, building an internal design wiki and running a motion design workshop; leading agendas for bi-weekly stand ups and design reviews; as well as managing the concepting and facilitation of photo shoots."[18] These processes improved efficiency and added huge value to Slack's bottom line by allowing designers to create meaningful brand experiences more quickly.

Collaboration In-house — Across Teams

In-house work allows opportunities to cultivate a shared sense of purpose within and across teams. But this can also present challenges. It requires collaborating with a client who is also a coworker. To establish a strong connection, Devin O'Bryan of IBM suggests dropping the "us vs. them" mentality. This is good advice for any creative team but particularly for those in-house who share with their client a common organizational commitment. Developing processes and strategies for cultivating collaboration across teams can produce not only a healthier working environment but also a more efficient workflow, and thus a stronger bottom line.

Collaboration In-house — Within Teams

Libby Bawcombe and Daniel Newman, who work as in-house design professionals for the NPR Digital Media Group, are well versed in agile processes. The design team shows work-in-progress, knowing that they may not have all the answers yet. The process is ongoing and the product is never truly finished. To foster conversation and collaboration, team members must be willing to share and work together closely on a day-to-day basis. Newman, who is director of product design, explains, "if you're someone who thrives working alone for long periods of time, this probably isn't the culture for you."[19] In-house work at NPR requires trust in the team and a commitment to figuring out the answers together.

The NPR design team has built an additional level of openness and collaboration by posting their own processes and ideas online at *Design at NPR: Stories from the design teams at National Public Radio*.[20] Bawcombe, manager of design research and strategy, who self-describes as an introvert, has explained that her work with the team has helped her to understand that collaboration is more productive when a wide variety of perspectives are heard, including those held by introverts. She even wrote an article about this for *Design at NPR*, in which she encourages introverts to speak up in conversation.[21] Acknowledging that this can be a challenge, she also places responsibility on the "steamrollers" (or more extroverted team members) to spend more time engaging introverts, listening, and stepping back to allow pauses—however awkward—so that others have a chance to speak up. On the same day that Bawcombe published her article, her colleague Veronica Erb published a piece from the perspective of the extrovert. In "How to Stop Steamrolling and Start Thinking Together," Erb encourages readers to pay attention to team dynamics so that they can see when they're steamrolling the team.[22] "As a person who tends to think *while* I speak," Erb writes, "I try to notice how I'm treating the people around me who think *and then* speak."[23] By writing about their communication process and strategy, Bawcombe and Erb demonstrate an openness that is essential to any well-functioning team.

Interview: Devin O'Bryan, IBM Design[24]

Devin O'Bryan has worked at IBM since 2014. Currently serving as design lead for IBM's Modeler Flows for Watson Studio, he started at IBM as the intern program lead when the company was just beginning to make huge investments in design.[25] Before coming to IBM, O'Bryan was a graphic design professor at Savannah College of Art and Design, and he was well positioned to integrate emerging designers into the IBM Design team and help them acclimate to working on a large, multifaceted creative team.

What are some differences between the work you do designing software at IBM and what you might see at a traditional design agency?

O'Bryan   An agency or consultancy ideates and incubates and then hands the work over and it gets taken care of in-house. When we do our process, we do everything here. The IBM loop never ends for software design. We are a lot more attached to the problems because the level of complexity is so massive and we don't hand off the project to the client.

What were some of the first challenges you faced when you began working at IBM?

O'Bryan   One of the first things was the "us vs. them" culture—us being design and them being engineering. We had to start really listening to our engineers and what they needed from us. It took time, but through this process we figured out how to effectively communicate with our engineering teams.

How did you resolve the challenge of collaborating with many different arms of the company?

O'Bryan   We would bring in whole engineering teams, management teams, and design product teams so those three voices were represented and we worked with a combination of agile methodologies and design thinking. When I began in 2014, we had something like one designer for every sixty-four engineers. Part of our work involved tempering the language around creativity so that engineers saw themselves as part of the team. My team developed bootcamps as an attempt to show engineers that they were some of the most creative people in the room.

What were you looking for in new team hires?

O'Bryan   I was looking for flexible people with flexible thought processes because we were defining a new process and workflow that hadn't been tested at our organization on such a large scale.

What are some common challenges that new designers face when joining a design team?

O'Bryan   When I first started at IBM, there were a lot of young professionals who didn't understand how to give or accept critique. Instead of making it about the work, they'd make it about the person, which isn't productive for collaboration. If you're going to grow you need to keep people receptive to things you have to say, not just be the loudest voice in the room.

What advice do you have for emerging creatives trying to navigate their way on a creative team?

O'Bryan   On a team, you've got to understand that as badly as you want it to be your idea, it's not your idea. It's the team's idea. It's the product of a lot of effort from a lot of people.

> ## CREATIVE WORKFLOWS
>
> Agile and waterfall processes are two of the most common design workflows used by creative teams. These are systemized ways of working that can be implemented in a wide range of creative tasks to improve outcomes and increase efficiency. Agile is an iterative approach to the design process. This means that teams can focus on improving a design over and over again in order to keep momentum moving forward. Waterfall, on the other hand, focuses on a linear progression of tasks that leads to the end goal of meeting a customer need. Because it doesn't focus on iteration, waterfall process can make it difficult to move back to a previous step in a project.
>
> Because of the flexibility, creative teams today are increasingly adopting agile processes. Though developed in the software design industry and then adopted by user experience design teams much like the ones discussed at NPR and IBM Design, a recent study showed that over 50 percent of in-house teams across creative sectors are now using agile or an agile/waterfall hybrid design process. This is a recent transformation; 69 percent of teams only started implementing agile processes in the past three years, suggesting that agile methods are beginning to replace older workflow models.[26]

Starting Out In-house

In-house work allows creatives the opportunity to see a brand develop over an extended period of time and build long-term relationships with different organizational teams. It can also offer reasonable hours (fewer than 45 a week[27]) and good benefits such as health care and paid time off. This is because in-house jobs typically don't require creatives to bill lots of hours to keep money coming in.

While working in-house can allow for a great work/life balance, this lifestyle often generates negative perceptions within the creative community. There's important work to be done in-house, even if creative professionals may not always see that value. As Professor Nida Abdullah observes, "I also think you are legitimized (if we're looking at the United States) by where you work. If you're working at a small school or you're in-house at a healthcare facility, that isn't legitimate or it's viewed as less than. I think that's where a lot of the hierarchy comes into play."[28] Abdullah complicates assumptions about hierarchy by pointing out how design is important across organizations and institutions, large and small. What's more, she argues that work at smaller organizations with a more local orientation can "expose you to the real ways design is part of people's lives."[29] In-house work, she suggests, can offer a new perspective on the power of design and its role in the world.

Interview: Thomas Harris and Gwendolyn Mumford, AIG Insurance[30]

Working as designers on a marketing team at AIG Insurance, Thomas Harris and Gwendolyn Mumford have experienced the ups and downs of working as in-house creatives. Both began in the company's travel division directly out of college and have since grown as designers and as communicators. They've learned the importance of being able to adapt and what it means to wear many hats within a single position.

What are the biggest challenges you face working on an in-house creative team?

Harris Our biggest challenge in the corporate in-house environment is for business leaders to understand how the creative team can be a strategic business partner. We don't only create visuals. We help facilitate client-focused strategies, elevate the way we position ourselves in the marketplace through proposals, and communicate one brand message.

Mumford I love working in-house because the brand identity is consistent, yet we have the opportunity to really push our brand boundaries and see where that takes us. But it can get a little stagnant and boring if we don't push each other to stay inspired. We have a good balance of projects, but there are often tedious tasks that don't inspire us. It helps that we not only take on projects that are specifically requested, but also come up with new ideas on our own.

What are some successes and failures you've experienced working on an in-house creative team?

Harris Successful moments include any time the team works proactively to develop campaigns and plan out creative strategies. Failure is when the team is exclusively reacting to what the business needs. There needs to be a balance in your work between proactive marketing and reacting to client/business needs.

Communication and processes for efficiency are all key factors for success. When we follow standard process and proactively plan campaigns or projects, the creative team excels. For instance, when our team communicated early and planned for the Global Business Travel Association (GBTA) conference, we developed an impactful campaign around our participation at the conference. By contrast, when we don't organize, we're faced with tight deadlines and a higher overall stress level.

Mumford I feel that Thomas and I communicate effectively regarding project delegation and management. (It also probably helps that we were friends before we were coworkers.) When it comes to projects involving the team as a whole—especially new types of projects—we often have communication issues. For instance, when we started expanding our social media, the content and responsibilities were vaguely defined. To prevent communication issues, we needed to clearly delegate tasks and define our process as a team.

Does your in-house team work with freelancers or outside agencies? If so, how do you balance those relationships?

Harris We have moved most of the work in-house but we do occasionally work with outside agencies. When projects are divided between in-house and agencies, the in-house group is only brought up to speed after a first draft is ready for us to review. We've worked with the account managers, but haven't been involved with the brainstorming processes or in contact with the agency creatives. For example, we work with one agency solely for video content. The AIG Travel marketing manager usually works with the agency account manager and copywriter to develop a script. Then the AIG Travel creative team will either develop the storyboard or closely review the agency's storyboard, and, once approved, the agency executes the animation or film and editing.

Mumford Our team used to work with more agencies and freelancers. From my perspective, a lot of the files that came from agencies and freelancers were inconsistent. It looked like different people from different companies had made them. It's easier to manage our brand with an in-house team. However, having agencies available is really helpful when we are busy and need someone who can commit their time directly to one project. I haven't spent too much time communicating with these agencies, but I know that my boss is in frequent communication to make sure everything they create aligns with our brand standards.

Do you worry about burnout and if so, how do you combat this?

Mumford Yes, I do worry about it. While I do feel that I have a good balance of fun projects and not-so-fun projects, when I have quick deadlines and tedious jobs it can get frustrating. We take screen breaks and walks around the AIG campus to keep frustration from building up. It helps to have fellow designers you know you can rely on.

Do you feel your work offers a good work/life balance on an in-house team?

Mumford I have a friend that graduated from school around the same time as me, and she works at an agency near our offices in Houston. She works later than I do, and it seems like they have crazier deadlines. I feel like we're pretty relaxed here. Of course, we do sometimes receive urgent projects from our boss, but I don't ever get anything that requires working nights or weekends.

Harris I do occasionally, but AIG corporate is really pushing a work/life balance initiative, which helps attract talented professionals to the company.

How do you stay inspired?

Harris I check creative blogs and keep reference materials handy—those college design books will forever be helpful. I'm really inspired by corporate graphic design from the early 1950s and 1960s so I try to find interesting examples online and apply similar techniques in a contemporary manner when designing for our brand.

Mumford Thomas and I recently started holding "inspiration" meetings. We'll take a few minutes out of our month to sit down and talk about designs we've seen or worked on that inspire us. I've really enjoyed doing this because it keeps me fresh to look at new design work without worrying about deadlines.

What advice do you have for emerging designers who are considering working on an in-house team?

Harris Expand your horizons. In-house creatives need to be able to design for print and digital, and also lead creative brainstorming sessions, write, code websites and emails, work in CMSs and email management systems, manage websites, understand and break down metric reporting/visually represent the data, and learn project management processes, marketing process, and marketing roles and responsibilities. Don't think that you can stay in your own lane and make an impact in the business.

Mumford Stay organized. Seriously. With multiple team members and teams from across the organization working on a project, we have to keep our server organized or we'd never be able to get things done. It's so frustrating when I can't easily edit a file due to poor organization. I also recommend interning as much as possible.

Working in-house as a design intern while I was still in school prepared me in a way that class projects just cannot do. Also: External hard drives will fail you, so invest in a solid-state drive and keep it in place so that you don't lose it.

How do you see creative teams developing in the future?

Harris   Today's creative teams are full of multifaceted individuals who take on business problems and use design thinking and creative tools to visually present solutions. I think the size of corporate branding teams is shrinking significantly. The new place for most designers is on new types of teams like the "science and technology" or "strategy, innovation, and customer experience" teams that manage a wide range of things including all-digital environments, the consistency of every customer's point-of-entry, and how we can innovate business processes.

Mumford   Based on my experience, I think the "design" role will continue to grow. For example, my title is "graphic designer," but I regularly work on social media. I'm constantly trying to develop more skills outside of design in order to bolster myself as a successful applicant in the future.

Challenges and Opportunities Working In-house

Working on an in-house creative team provides many challenges and opportunities. Though in-house work is often perceived as stagnant or lacking creativity, this chapter has shown that there are numerous opportunities for in-house team members to use their deep organizational knowledge to shape brand development and strategy over time.

While in-house creative teams can be misunderstood by an organization's other arms and viewed as a service provider instead of a strategic partner, initiatives like the Inside Out Awards are helping to change this by elevating the work of in-house creative teams. On the ground, there are many strategies for improving relationships across teams. These include setting clear expectations and developing systems and processes for coordinating work across an organization's different arms.

These efforts make a difference. The value of in-house teams is becoming more widely recognized, and in-house teams are growing at a time when agency teams are seeing decline. But it's not an either/or situation. Rather, when an in-house team doesn't have the capabilities to do all the creative work themselves, they'll outsource to an agency, meaning that the two often have to work together. This can be an opportunity to collaborate and share expertise.

In-house teams need members who will rally around their brand and work to elevate it in the marketplace over a long period of time. Such positions also tend to offer a good work/life balance and an opportunity to really commit to a brand and invest in the real impact design can have on people's lives.

EXERCISE: UNDERSTANDING AN IN-HOUSE BRAND

Now that you've learned about the challenges and opportunities of working on an in-house creative team, you can use this exercise to dig deeper into an in-house team of your choosing.

Step 1: Select an Industry
Start by selecting an industry where you would like to make an impact. For instance, are you passionate about helping people? There are many non-profit organizations such as UNICEF that have robust in-house creative teams. Do you love sports? Most major sports teams employ in-house marketing and creative teams, and there are many companies that make sporting goods and apparel. You could also research media outlets for sports reporting as well as non-profit sports initiatives.

Step 2: Focus Your Work Style
Now that you've identified an industry, consider the following: Are you interested in working with a large global brand or with an organization committed to local impact? Or do you want to see the impact of your design in your own community through a local or regional brand?

Step 3: Make a List
Assemble a list of organizations or companies that fit your determined profile and that you're interested in learning more about. To build your network, narrow your scope to your local region or regions where you might like to move. Now, find out if the companies on your short list have an in-house creative team, and select one to research further.

Step 4: Narrow and Research
Once you have selected a brand that you're excited to learn more about, research its in-house creative team. See if you can find more information to answer the following preparatory questions:

How large is the team?

Does their website highlight any projects they've created?

What types of roles are on the team?

Does your skill set and area of expertise complement or grow the team's?

Step 5: Analyze a Project

Now, select a project created by your selected in-house creative team and analyze it by answering the following questions:

What was the goal of the project?

Do you think the project was successful? Why or why not?

Did the project have measurable outcomes? If so, what are they and how does that impact your perception of the project?

What's attractive about working on a project like this? What's less desirable?

Step 6: Conduct an Interview

If you can find an in-house creative team member to contact within the organization, consider reaching out and asking for a 20-minute discovery phone call to get their take on the project. You can ask the team member the same questions about the project that you answered. Consider also talking to them about in-house creative work more generally, asking questions such as:

What are the benefits of working for an in-house brand?

What are the challenges of working on an in-house creative team?

How does creative work you do impact the organization?

Step 7: Record Your Discoveries

Last, write down your discoveries. How did your analysis compare with what you learned in your interview with the team member?

4 FREELANCE TEAMS

Vanessa Carney was a copywriter at a large digital marketing agency in New York City when she realized she wanted to pivot to a career as a freelancer. Freelancers would routinely come through the office for the fun part of projects like the pitches and the brainstorming, but rarely stayed for the grunt work that followed. That was her job. To her, these freelancers seemed like rock stars, constantly honing their craft without having to deal with internal politics. "They really just had to worry about writing and coming up with ideas, or designing the thing. They didn't have to attend internal status meetings or attend reviews. They were brought in to do a job and then they left. That really appealed to me."[1] Carney also noticed freelancers had more flexibility in their schedules. "Their schedule was respected, like the team leader might say, 'Dave has to work from Montreal for a week, is that cool?' And I thought, 'Wow, yeah that's cool.'"[2] The opportunity to dictate work/life balance independently was another appealing draw to the freelance lifestyle. With five years of full-time agency experience behind her, Carney gave up her steady paycheck and made the leap into the freelance world.

Freelance Creative "Teams"

In the twenty-first century, creative professionals have access to technologies that help make freelancing easier than ever before. There are numerous software solutions to help manage a freelancer's many responsibilities, including finances, contracts, client lists, emails, social media, and promotion. On top of that, designers can work with a lean set of tools stripped down to a laptop computer and the latest creative software. With a "work from anywhere" mindset and a technology that is keeping pace with excellent tools for the creative entrepreneur, working for oneself is well within reach.

But freelancing isn't all fun. Freelancers must be adept at working both independently and collaboratively. Paul Jarvis, author of *Company of One*, a guidebook to running a minimalist business, writes that freelancers must have a specific skill set. "On a team, it's easier to be motivated because there are more immediate repercussions."[3] The collective nature of working on a team makes it easier to stay on task. By contrast, freelancers are often doing the work independently. This requires internal motivation to do the work.

According to staffing company Robert Half, companies face many challenges when hiring freelancers.[4] Some of the most common issues reported by managers and art directors include negotiating pay rates, finding skilled freelancers, making them feel like part of the team, communicating or collaborating effectively with them, and getting them up to speed quickly. Freelancers can resolve these challenges with effective communication skills and accountability. For example, freelancers can go out of their way to meet the team they are working with. Meeting up for a coffee or a video chat with individual members of the team can help a freelancer integrate. By learning about individual team members' responsibilities, freelancers can learn how the team works and figure out how to best serve the client, which could be an agency. Developing close professional ties with a client may increase opportunities for repeat work. This is a great way for freelancers to bring in consistent income, which can be a challenge at any time, but particularly when starting out.

To ensure accountability, freelancers must develop techniques and work habits that work for them. Though different people have different strategies, it can often be useful to define a workspace, even if working from home. This might be a dedicated home office, a kitchen table, or a bedroom nook. But wherever it is, clear the space free from distraction and make a ritual of setting it up for "work time" versus "home time," so that it's easier to cultivate a workday mindset when on the clock. Preventing inadvertent distraction may require clear communication with others sharing the space, especially about when the workday begins and when it ends.

While some freelancers struggle with distraction, others wrestle with overwork. Without a clear line between work time and time off, it can be easy to end up working all hours of the day. It's important to set work hours and include regular breaks. If possible, schedule some time outside the house to take a walk or grab something to eat. This can help manage the feeling of isolation that can come with working from home. Local or virtual creative professional groups can be a good tool for staying connected with like-minded creative professionals. They can also be used to grow professional networks and exchange creative ideas and freelancing strategies.

It's hard to know how to charge clients for creative work, especially when starting out. While offering low rates may seem like a great way to begin getting clients, this can diminish perceptions of the value of creative work and negatively impact other freelance professionals. There are many resources that offer recommendations for how to price freelance work. For instance, in the United States, the Graphic Artists Guild provides its own handbook on pricing and ethical guidelines. Updated annually, the book has hundreds of pages covering topics such as business practices, income, and pricing for various creative industries, legal rights, contracts, and more.[5] Many organizations and creative professionals are also beginning to share their knowledge and pricing strategies to help other freelancers navigate the pricing process.[6] There is even a call for more transparency in sharing salary data and freelance rates among creative professionals.[7] This can help eliminate gender pay gaps and empower creative professionals to negotiate for better pay. While freelancers tend to work on an hourly basis, as opposed to a salary, it can help to understand the rates for both freelance and full-time professionals. Freelancers must factor in not only basic pay, but also the cost of covering their own benefits and ancillary costs such as a computer and creative software required to do their work. Getting informed about pay rates and business costs is an important step to becoming a successful freelancer.

Record keeping is also very important for building a successful career as a freelancer. It requires tracking hours and taking note of how time is spent working for each client. Invoices should detail this information so that clients know what they are paying for. It's also important to track receipts and keep clear accounting records. There are many great software tools for project management, time keeping, contracts, invoices, and accounting, and it's often worth exploring and testing a few different programs to determine what works best. Freelancing permits great independence, but to be successful also requires developing workable systems and processes.

Different Ways to Freelance

A creative freelance career can take many shapes, and there are many different ways to freelance. In some cases, freelancing is a direct-to-client business, which means running the entire creative process from start to finish, much like an agency. In other cases, agencies hire freelancers to develop creative work for a client on a short-term basis. In-house teams also hire freelance professionals to assist with projects.

When working direct-to-client, freelancers can set their own schedules with the client's team without an intermediary. This can streamline project communication, allowing the freelancer to set boundaries and manage client expectations. Direct-to-client often means you can work from anywhere you like. Though remote work is becoming increasingly common across all sectors of business and the need for in-person meetings less necessary, depending on the client's preferences, direct-to-client work may still require in-office meetings or presentations. One of the most challenging aspects of direct-to-client work is finding new clients, because freelancers may be overshadowed by more robust agency teams. A great way to build up a client list is to specialize in an area that may be underserved, such as small businesses or non-profits. Building a great reputation in a particular sector can lead to referrals and inquiries from new clients.

While direct-to-client work allows freelancers to work independently, freelancing for an agency involves working as part of a creative team and reporting to a manager (usually the art director or creative director for the client). Agencies typically bring on freelancers to fill a specific role or provide a specific skill such as design work, copywriting, or custom illustration. The art director often already has a client brief to anchor the project and may even bring on a freelancer after the project is underway. Depending on the agency's preferences and needs, the work may be carried out remotely or on-site, in the same office as the team. Freelance work with agencies requires flexibility to establish a good workflow with the full-time creative team and, to stay on task, efficiency in working methods.

Freelancers also sometimes join in-house creative teams to fill out roles in areas for which the company doesn't have full-time creative staff. In-house teams value a freelancer's specialized skill set and the flexibility to hire them as needed.

Regardless of the kind of freelance work you choose to take on, the same principles of teamwork apply: it's important to be reliable, a strong communicator, committed to the team's success, and responsible for taking initiative. Making sure these skills become part of your personal brand will ensure that clients keep coming back to you for freelance work.

Developing a Style

Designers must often be chameleons, varying their work to suit a client and the demands of a specific creative problem. While most freelance designers build their reputations by creating consistently high-quality work with great attention to detail, illustrators often establish theirs by developing a recognizable style. (This is also often true of photographers and those working in hand lettering.) Developing a personal style is a hotly debated topic in the creative world, and there are pros and cons to it. Illustrators with a personal style must be able to showcase a variety of work in one style so that clients can see the flexibility of the technique for a range of applications. Illustrators working in multiple illustration styles must create a portfolio that includes many examples within each style to show that they can replicate the style again and again and the client knows they will get that same quality for their project.

Freelance illustrator Steve Simpson found that when he first started working full-time for an animation studio, his ability to work in many styles was an asset. When he made the transition to freelance, he had to shift gears and try to find his own voice by developing a unique style. "I suddenly realized that I didn't have one style," he remembers. "I had a million styles and none of them was my own."[8] With prior experience in comics, Simpson began working in a cartoon style during his early illustration career and he has since refined the look and feel of his graphics so that they are easily recognizable as his. Simpson notes the importance of this for illustrators in particular, because many companies don't hire full-time illustrators.

When new to the field, it's difficult to get work seen by art directors and editors. "I encourage illustrators to go work in design studios doing a broad range of creative work," he says. "Try to spend those first couple years within the creative industry."[9] This strategy permits time to learn about the creative process from within an agency and get to know more about how agencies contract freelance illustrators and other creative professionals. However, it also means less time to develop a personal style, and thus requires devoting more personal time to developing an illustration portfolio and taking on small side projects to gain more recognition as an illustrator.

Building Connections

Cultivating a Network

A freelancer's most important asset is their reputation, and the only way to cultivate and build a strong reputation is through a professional network. This is important in all areas of business, but for the freelancer, network is king. Every freelancer featured in this chapter emphasized the importance of building a strong network before setting out independently. While it's important to create high-quality work within realistic deadlines, the value of this is only worth something if people know it's available.

A good way to start building a network is through school connections and alumni relations. These relationships can be cultivated with peers in school by keeping in touch and sharing work with one another. Many classmates will go on to work full-time in companies that will need freelance help. Most colleges and universities maintain alumni networks and reaching out through these channels can also yield help from more experienced professionals who are interested in connecting with emerging talent from their alma mater. Because networking opportunities can often pop up unexpectedly, it's useful to be ready to talk about your work and your skills. Consider preparing a short pitch that you can use when people ask about your work.

The most reliable way to get freelance work is through referrals. No matter the career phase, building a strong reputation is vital to success. This may involve sustaining strong relationships; being kind, open, and positive; and delivering high-quality work on time. Building a strong reputation is an ongoing task, and it's important to always focus on professionalism as a key component of a strong professional identity.

Social Media

Social media can be a great way to share work. Many artists, designers, illustrators, and hand letterers promote themselves through multiple online channels. Instagram, Dribbble, and even LinkedIn are strong platforms for promoting creative work, but illustrator Steve Simpson recommends Behance, a popular platform specifically designed for showcasing and discovering creative work. "I got onto Behance very early back in 2010," he remembers, "and now I have a big following there, which makes it easier to get noticed."[10]

The landscape of social media constantly evolves, and it's important to analyze and take stock of what's working and what isn't. Focus time and energy accordingly.

Agents

Many illustrators and hand lettering artists work with agents who bring them client work. There are pros and cons to working with an agent. On the one hand, they can be useful, particularly for those who are just starting out, because agents have direct connections to companies that purchase artwork. But their service comes at a price; agents often take a percentage of earnings. When working with an agent, it's important to be clear about ambitions and expectations. Be specific about the type of work you're willing to take on and what you're unwilling to do. If a designer turns down too many jobs or doesn't produce enough new work, agents will stop showing their portfolio, so the more transparency around expectations the better. Working with an agent is a business relationship, and requires a contract with terms laid out. Be sure to review all the details carefully and consider seeking legal advice before committing.

Passion Projects

One of the most positive aspects of freelancing is being able to make time for passion projects. These can also offer an opportunity to develop a personal brand and cultivate a following, which can, in turn, help attract new clients. Hand lettering artist Jessica Hische gained traction early in her career by launching a site called Daily Drop Cap where she posted a new illustrated drop cap every day. (A drop cap is a capital letter that's enlarged and decorated to add emphasis for the reader.) This site helped people learn about her work.[11] Now, Hische is considered a leading voice in her field. One-a-day projects are a great way for all designers to push creative boundaries and refine skills. And as Hische's story shows, projects like these can accelerate career development.

Awards and Professional Societies

Awards are a long tradition in art and design and can be another great way to earn peer recognition and get noticed by potential clients and art directors. Many designers and illustrators submit to annual awards such as Communication Arts, 3x3, Creative Quarterly, and Graphic Design USA, to name just a few. Award-winning designs are published online or included in printed annuals, where many industry professionals look to find new creative talent. While it may take time to build the skills to win top awards, it's worth investigating categories that support students or emerging creative talent. Whether or not you win, submitting to awards can help boost confidence and generate visibility for your work.

Promoting Your Work Offline

While professional portfolio websites are a popular way to showcase creative abilities, there are also ways to promote work offline. For instance, it's not uncommon for illustrators to send postcards of their work to art directors. It's also good practice to have business cards, which can showcase your design and creative talents while also helping you connect with peers and potential clients. Consider developing a brochure of services to mail to various local businesses that may utilize your design talents. It also helps to develop a portfolio that's just as easy to email as a pdf as to print off and present in an interview or pitch meeting.

Making connections and building a robust professional network takes a lot of work. Networks are not readymade. They're built over time. A strong work ethic and an ability to self-promote will go a long way towards helping you to build those important connections throughout your career.

Freelance Workflows

When freelancers are hired, they can be brought onto creative teams in a variety of ways. If doing work for a small company, the freelancer might work as a team of one. For example, Steve Simpson recalls a package design project where he worked directly with the owner of the company that hired him. Simpson came up with the ideas, created the artwork, and, once the owner approved them, sent the files to the printer.

In other cases, the project can involve a lot of moving pieces. For example, consider a scenario in which a client approaches a creative agency for a project. The team comes up with ideas and pitches them to the client. Once an idea is approved, a freelancer might be brought in to execute the aspects of the project that require their creative skills. In some cases, selected freelancers will pitch their ideas, much like advertising agencies, to win the project. Although common, some professionals frown on this practice unless it is a paid pitch, where the freelancer is compensated for their time, regardless of whether or not they win the pitch. Freelance professionals must decide for themselves if they're willing to participate in a process like this.

Once a freelancer has been hired by a creative team, they are often presented with an idea that is quite specific and must be executed under very explicit instructions. While it's important to follow a creative brief, it's okay to ask for more creative control and get a sense of whether or not the client is open to hearing more ideas. For example, Steve Simpson found that he was able to gain more control over the creative process when he began doing his own hand lettering within his illustrations. "The reason I do design as well as illustration," he says, is to "have more quality control over the final result. This is based on an experience early in my career where my illustrations were paired with Comic Sans [an informal typeface based on comic book lettering] and it was too late for me to do anything about it."[12] After this, he got up the nerve to ask the client directly if he could do the typography himself and was surprised when the client agreed without hesitation. While creative workflows can be very clearly defined, it's okay to ask for more creative input, particularly if you think you can improve the quality of the final product.

CASE STUDY: JAMESON WHISKEY: COLLABORATING AS A FREELANCE ILLUSTRATOR

Freelance professionals may work for themselves, but they do collaborate when working on a creative project. In this case study, a freelance project shows how agencies, clients, and freelancers work together to complete a project.

Project
Jameson Whiskey limited edition bottle packaging design by Steve Simpson[13]

Client
Jameson

Creative Team
Agency: Design Bridge
Illustrator: Steve Simpson

Duration
2013–2015, 21 months total

Description
In this project, freelance illustrator Steve Simpson developed the fifth annual limited edition label for Jameson's 2015 St. Patrick's Day whiskey bottle.

The client, Jameson, wanted to represent the city of Dublin on its limited edition bottle to celebrate the fact that Jameson was first distilled in Dublin in 1780. Simpson describes the positive experience he had working on this project because it allowed for significant creative freedom:

"I was asked to create a label that represented what Dublin meant to me and was give the freedom to focus on what I love about the city."[14]

The St. Patrick's Day limited edition bottle annually features custom artwork highlighting Irish culture with a design that is distinct from the traditional Jameson packaging. This limited edition product generates customer excitement for the brand year after year.

Process

This was a collaboration between Jameson, Simpson, and London-based agency Design Bridge. Design Bridge began the process by assembling a long list of reputable and talented illustrators, and then narrowed down the list to their top three choices. These three illustrators, among them Simpson, did a paid pitch and submitted their ideas for consideration.

FIGURE 4.1 Jameson pencil rough sketch by Steve Simpson.

Steve Simpson was inspired by the welcoming city of Dublin when he started creating his design for the Jameson limited edition bottle; the project took twenty-one months from this initial concept to the finished product.

Simpson's design was inspired by his move to Dublin in 1990. "My first impressions of Dublin were extremely welcoming," he remembers. "You can go into a bar and within five minutes be best friends with the person sitting next to you, and there's nowhere else like it in the world."[15]

Incorporating local slang and city landmarks in Simpson's signature whimsical style that blends hand-lettered text and image, the design prominently features a custom rendition of the Jameson logo on Dublin's O'Connell bridge with angel wings on either side and the tagline, "Wherever I roam. Dublin, my heart calls home."

Outcome

Once Simpson was selected to create the 2015 limited edition label, he refined the concept put forth in his sketch and went through many revisions of every detail. He even gave special attention to the barcode, which resembles the General Post Office, a recognizable Dublin building.

Daniel Lundberg, global brand director for Jameson, reflected on the strong fit between Simpson's unique design and the Jameson brand. "Jameson is synonymous with its hometown of Dublin," he observes. "Both are steeped in heritage, have infectious, welcoming personalities and are leaders in contemporary craft, so this limited edition bottle is our way of paying homage to this great city."[16] The design was also recognized with a Bronze Bell for packaging design at ICAD2015.

Questions for Thought

What are your thoughts about developing a personal style? Do you feel it's necessary in your work?

Are there any artists you follow with a recognizable style? What makes it distinct?

Would you be open to pitching in order to win a freelance project? Why or why not?

FIGURE 4.2 Final designs.

The final design of the label missing caption.

FIGURE 4.3 Front and back labels.

The front and back bottle labels showcase local knowledge of Dublin through maps, icons, and song lyrics. There's even a nod to local architecture in the barcode design.

FIGURE 4.4 Final product.

The label design is centered around a heart, which encapsulates Simpson's feelings about Dublin, where he felt instantly at home. In the end, he treated the project as if he was creating a label for himself, but it also resonated with the larger Jameson audience and spoke to many people's warm feelings towards Dublin.

FIGURE 4.5 Collaboration diagram.

Despite being a freelance illustrator who works for himself, Steve Simpson has to collaborate with a team on almost every creative project. In this project, he worked alongside a creative agency to develop the work for the client, Jameson.

The Art Director/Copywriter Freelance Team

When art director Kristen Curtis and copywriter Aldo Arias met while working at an advertising agency in New York City, they hit it off and decided to freelance together, creating their own company, Only Child. Their partnership is distinct from an agency in that they don't do direct-to-client work. Instead, agencies or production companies contract them either individually or as a team. Curtis had worked as a freelancer previously and was always getting paired up with copywriters. "It seemed like an advantage to come as a package deal," she recalls, "and it's worked out really well."[17] When they collaborate with an agency or a production company on a job, they're able to deliver better work for the client because they already have a well-oiled working relationship. Operating much like the traditional art director/copywriter teams of the Bernbach days discussed in Chapter 1, Curtis and Arias's partnership has allowed Only Child to carve out a unique space in the freelance market because clients can hire them as a package deal, knowing they already have chemistry and a history of great ideas. But while they typically collaborate on projects, clients don't have to hire them both. If, for example, a client has budget concerns, they can hire either Curtis or Arias, depending on their needs.

The partnership has been particularly useful for Curtis, who has observed obstacles to developing a freelance career as a woman creative. She points out that the advertising industry is still a boys' club, and it helps to have a man on the team. When clients don't listen, Curtis has Arias to back her up. "It's a sad reality," she says, "but it helps get my ideas heard."[18]

Only Child's small size and forward-thinking mentality have allowed the company to stay nimble. They've found a niche in the production world and stay on top of the technological trends in experiential and social advertising. As Curtis observes, "some of the big agencies seem incapable of updating. For instance, we were working on a social campaign and the executive creative director asked to see the print ad ... they just can't interpret the work."[19] As a team, they use their agility and understanding of the digital trends in advertising to accommodate and educate clients on how to use exciting new strategies to drive business forward.

Interview: Kristen Curtis and Aldo Arias, Only Child[20]

Curtis and Arias have great advice for how solo or team freelancers can keep learning and evolving to stay relevant and serve clients in innovative ways.

How do you start freelancing with a new team?

Curtis You have to build a lot of trust in a very short amount of time so you don't have people questioning your decision making. We're coming in at a higher level and have to delegate to people who have worked for the client for a long time and feel like they have more authority.

Arias Getting in the mindset of showing up and staying focused and figuring out exactly how everyone else around you works and what exactly they're looking for. You're joining a preexisting structure, but it's your job to figure out what's needed to get the work done because in a lot of cases the client doesn't know or hasn't planned it. It's pretty common for us to plan out the strategy ourselves and tell the team, "Let's do it this way."

How do you gain the trust of a team?

Arias I think one important tool is to ask the questions that no one is asking. There is a culture of fear around not knowing, so rather than asking, people will just give it their best shot and get it wrong from the get-go. There is a logic to that, because in these agencies you can be punished for asking questions and showing gaps in knowledge. But as a freelancer, you can ask these questions and no one is going to fire you. In fact, people will really appreciate seeing that willingness to probe.

Curtis I would also say never underestimate the power of lunch. No one takes it, everyone eats at their desk. It really helps to just invite someone to lunch. It really goes a long way to build trust with their team. It seems obvious but it helps.

What advice can you give to emerging designers interested in freelancing?

Curtis Stand up for yourself. It's difficult at first if you don't know when that next paycheck is coming, but you don't need to take attitude at work.

Arias Get a full-time job at an agency for a year or two. At school, you can learn protocol and procedures and build a portfolio, but managing personal relationships, personalities, and politicking in a company structure is something you can only learn on the job. Find someone senior who you like and just learn everything you can from them, because they know how to play the game.

Curtis There is a lack of mentorship in advertising, but finding someone that is a bit more senior and wants to take you under their wing, that really does help. Working at an agency also helps to temper expectations of what you're supposed to do coming out of school and how you're actually utilized at an agency. It's a bit of a shock. At first you think you're going to come in and be able to pitch giant ideas and create amazing campaigns and that's just not the reality. There's a hierarchy in place that you have to navigate and, like Aldo said, it's good to learn how to navigate it all before you go out into the freelance world.

Arias Plus, at the agency, you make the connections and find the people who will be looking for you when you want to freelance. Advertising is set up for freelancers. In other industries, it's not always an option. There's an infrastructure here for it to work. I think everyone should try freelancing, even if only to gain more perspective on your full-time work.

Freelance Collectives

Not all freelancer teams are structured as a partnership in which the team comes as a package deal. Collectives like Ghostly Ferns, Gifted Creative Group, and The Neverwoods offer another model for freelance collaboration. In this model, members work together on a per project basis and curate the talent that is the best fit for the project. Creatives can be hired individually, but if the client requires it, the structure also provides opportunity to work as a group, as would happen at an agency. This way, a client looking for illustration and user experience services can hire two members of the collective as a team. Because members of the collective know and trust each other, and can hit the ground running on a new job, collectives are well positioned to compete with agencies for more complex creative projects that might otherwise be out of reach. This model allows freelancers to maintain their autonomy and control their own client work, but also offers opportunities to work on larger projects and build lasting working relationships with other creative professionals.

When entering into any partnership with friends or creative colleagues, it's important to legitimize the partnership with clear guidelines and a signed contract that dictates rates and expectations for each member of the team. As with an agent, it may be worth consulting a lawyer or online legal service to clarify the terms of the partnership to avoid difficulties if there are disagreements later.

The Freelancer and Client Team

Not everyone thinks of their client as part of their team, but the best freelancers treat them as such. Approaching the client as a team member is a great way to build trust in the working relationship. Graphic designer and full-time freelancer, Christy Batta, works with non-profits and businesses doing good for others and she values her clients as crucial to the design process. She sees the advantage in working directly with clients one-on-one rather than working as part of a larger agency where many designers may have a hand in the project. Most of Batta's clients view this as a benefit. "It's very different for someone to work with an individual designer than an agency," she says. "With me, my clients know when they call they're always going to get me and be able to contact me directly. I've talked to people who say they don't like working with an agency because they just don't know what to expect or who's going to get the project done."[21]

One of Batta's favorite clients to work with is a non-profit called National Industries for the Blind. "They see a graphic design consultant as a valuable team member and this is how it should be."[22] Because of the trust that Batta has built with organization, she's allowed to be more creative and have more freedom in the projects. The end result is a strong design that meets the client's business needs and results in more future work with that client. Batta says that it also allows her to "be a better version" of herself.[23]

Sometimes freelancers must work hard to build trust with a new client who has been burned by designers in the past. Batta has a technique for getting through this. When she has an initial call with a client, she asks them if they've worked with designers in the past and how it went. Learning about what worked in a previous experience or what failed can help Batta ensure a positive relationship with the client going forward.

Trust is also established through reliability. Paul Jarvis started out with a good roster of clients based on his connections from the agency world, but when it came to keeping those clients, it was a matter of meeting his deadlines. This, he says, is where many creatives seem to fail. "I stood out because I did my work and I communicated well, especially when there was a problem," he observes.[24] Some creatives struggle with time management, and in these cases, freelance work may not be the best option. In addition to great communication and a strong work ethic, it's important to understand time management because much of a freelancer's time is spent on business development such as contracts, invoicing, marketing, and self-promotion. It's important to understand a client's experiences early on and try to reset their expectations so they know they're in good hands. References and testimonials from prior clients can also be a great way to reassure new ones.

Freelancers Need Coaching Too

The life of a freelancer can be lonely. Running a business and hunting for new clients can be exhausting. It's important to know when to bring in help. While there are countless resources and webinars available online, there are also people who do this for their job. When Christy Batta decided it was time to level up in her business, she looked to brand and business coach, Maggy Sterner. Before launching her career as a coach, Sterner worked on the NPR digital team when the web was brand new. While there, she realized that she most enjoyed the earliest phase of creating a website, the part she calls "discovery," where you find out what you're building, who it's for, and why. This is exactly what she does as a coach. "You can look at the core of what are you trying to do and translate it from jargon, or take it from a million words to pithy, short, powerful statements that describe what you're really up to. I thought that project of discovery was so interesting."[25]

Now a trained and certified coach, Sterner describes her role as that of a translator, helping her clients to put their ideas into clear language that *their* clients will also understand. "In their hearts they know, but it's in their blind spots. I'm like an archeologist and I dig it out for them."[26] For Batta, Sterner worked on her pain points, including controlling the narrative surrounding her business. Batta wanted to be able to describe the most important pieces of her design practice, but she struggled to find the words. Over the course of six months, Sterner coached her to figure out answers to the following important questions:

- Who are you?
- What do you stand for?
- What's the vision for your business?
- What separates you from the competition?
- Who's the ideal client?

After she'd developed answers to these questions, Batta worked to create an elevator pitch, brand positioning statements, website, and social media content. Then she implemented and tested these in the world. Batta, like most of Sterner's best clients, had been in business for over a year and had exhausted other resources such as the endless virtual webinars. By the time they began working together, Batta knew what she needed from Sterner. Because she was somewhat established before bringing on a coach, Batta also had the financial resources to cover the cost.

Without a boss and a team to drive business development, it's easy to put it on the back burner. As Batta states, "When you're freelance, it's hard to prioritize that stuff in your schedule."[27] Many different kinds of coaching are available to freelancers, including career consulting, business coaching, wellness coaching, and technical training. It's always important to consider needs and pain points to identify what will be most useful moving forward.

From Freelancer to Entrepreneur

In his book *Company of One*, Paul Jarvis argues that there is a difference between a freelancer and what he terms a "company of one." "While freelancing is a perfect first step to becoming a company of one," he writes, freelancers "exchange time for money."[28] In other words, if they're not working, they're not getting paid. While freelancers get paid per hour, project, or deliverable, a company of one is an entrepreneur that utilizes systems and automations to build a business that can sustain and make money, even when time is not spent working. Both freelancers and companies of one work for themselves. But, as Jarvis explains, in a company of one, "you're not trading time for money, but instead operating and profiting outside of the time you spend working and beyond your one-to-one relationships."[29]

Jarvis began as a freelancer before creating a company where he does not have to manage any employees or punch a clock. Since starting his business in the 1990s, he has resisted the growth mindset that is prevalent in business. While he watched his friends head up agencies and deal with hard economic times that required tough decisions such as layoffs, his one-man operation could ride out economic downturns and bounce back quickly. Although he is a great collaborator and communicator, Jarvis is not interested in building a team. Instead, he collaborates on a per project basis, which allows for flexibility and frees him from having to manage other people—a task he's never wanted to do. Instead of expanding into an agency to meet his web design clients' growing demand, he found ways to optimize his offerings and charge more for his services without having to work more or hire a team.

Jarvis's entrepreneurial mindset allowed him to optimize his workflow and make more money without feeling overworked. Other ways that designers can develop passive income streams include:

- Selling digital templates for online marketplaces such as Etsy and Creative Market.
- Teaching online creative courses on platforms such as Skillshare, Teachable, and Udemy.
- Selling custom-designed merchandise such as stickers and clothing.

The Freelance Life

Vanessa Carney has been working as a freelance copywriter in New York City since 2013 and the flexibility and lifestyle has lived up to her imagination. Although still hard work, freelancing allows Carney to focus on her craft. Her time is dedicated to developing high-quality content for clients, and isn't bogged down with agency politics. She often works remotely, giving her more autonomy over her schedule. This allows her to create a work/life balance that suits her needs. While work is usually steady, Carney suggests having savings to fall back on when work gets slow.[30] Experts typically advise those setting out on their own to have six to twelve months of savings in the bank to cover expenses. For most, this is a tall order, so consider freelancing part-time while working another job. This can be a good way to test the waters.

Freelancing requires taking risks. But many creative professionals find that these risks are far outweighed by the rewards. Freelancers create the type of life they want through a more balanced daily schedule, finding and taking time for projects that inspire passion. There are many ways to a fulfilling creative career. Freelancing is one of many options.

EXERCISE: EXAMINING YOUR WORK HABITS

As a freelancer, it's particularly important to build self-discipline around your schedule and work habits. Whether you're a morning person or a night owl, you must figure out a work habit that suits both you and your clients. This exercise is about tracking your work habits to identify strengths and weaknesses. If you're not freelancing yet, this is a great way to discover whether or not it's a good fit for you.

Step 1: Develop a Project

Develop a self-directed project with a one- to four-week timeline. This should focus on an area that you'd like to pursue professionally. Here are some example projects to consider:

a. Create one full-page editorial illustration to complement a recent news article. Timeline: 2 weeks.
b. Develop a social media strategy and copywriting to promote a new product launch. Timeline: 1 week.
c. Develop a logo and eight-plus page brand guide for a local non-profit. Timeline: 3 weeks.
d. Create a wire frame and prototype of a ten-page website for a new e-commerce company. Timeline: 4 weeks.

Step 2: Develop a Brief

Once you've selected a project to complete, make sure you write out the specific goals you will accomplish so you have a clear creative brief to anchor your work.

Step 3: Schedule Your Time

Estimate how long it will take to complete your project and develop a schedule for completion. Start by mapping out the various steps involved and how much each of those will take so that you can budget time accordingly and track your progress carefully. Be specific with dates and times that you will work, which all lead to a final date on which you will deliver the work (e.g., Monday—Begin project, work from 6 p.m. to 8 p.m.). As you develop your schedule, consider what you would expect to make as an hourly rate for this project and start to develop a budget for what you'd charge if you were billing a client for this work.

Step 4: Begin Your Project

Once you've scheduled your project, use it to begin work. As you proceed, track your progress and discoveries. For example, note any challenges or new strategies you develop as you work. Track your time every day you work on the project, and make sure to be honest in your reporting so you can have an accurate assessment of your work habits at the end of the project.

Step 5: Finish the Project and Reflect

Once your deadline arrives, reflect on the process.

> Were you able to complete the project?
>
> Did it take more or less time than expected?
>
> Did you find you could balance the project with a job and/or school work?
>
> Did you stick to your schedule?
>
> Did you find it difficult to focus?
>
> Did you develop any new strategies or work habits?
>
> Did you enjoy the process of being able to dictate your schedule and manage your own project?

Working on self-directed creative projects is a great way to build up a portfolio of work you'd like to do for clients, but this exercise is also focused on examining work habits. Many creative professionals start out working full-time for an employer and this structure can be really valuable to developing great work habits. If you found it difficult to motivate yourself, freelance work might be something to hold off on for now. But if you enjoyed working for yourself and don't mind the deadline pressure, consider trying out freelance work. Keep working hard to build a portfolio and focus on networking to find those first clients that will get you started.

5 COMMUNITY AS AN EXTENSION OF CREATIVE TEAM

When Sarah Obenauer was considering a career transition, she looked to her community of local creative professionals for support and asked questions. At the same time as she was reflecting on her own career path and past experience working for non-profit organizations, she learned the creative professionals in her network wanted to find their place in the creative community. They also wanted a way to use their creative skills to better their wider local community. Obenauer started to define a problem that she wanted to solve: "I saw the impact of good design, but also the difficulties faced by community organizations that can't afford to hire someone."[1] Sarah Obenauer and her husband Alexander Obenauer found a way to bridge the gap between non-profit and creative communities through the creation of Make a Mark, a twelve-hour design and development marathon benefitting humanitarian causes. Obenauer believes that the project's success comes from the understanding and appreciation between creative teammates. It's this that allows maker teams to develop in twelve hours a project that would normally take months to complete. Understanding and appreciation is also what helped Obenauer to develop this project as a full-time career. She used the support and ideas from her existing creative community to build a new community that stretches across the globe.

Community as Creative Team

Whether or not you're currently employed, you can think of your existing professional and creative community as your creative team. Cultivate those relationships and find ways to collaborate to strengthen that community and make it grow. The benefits of growing a creative community are numerous. Cultivating and expanding a creative community offer opportunities to build a network, which may lead to new and interesting career openings that otherwise would have been unavailable. New connections can also lead to lasting relationships with peers in a similar phase of their career, and other creative professionals in different stages. Building a robust creative community may yield a mentor, or provide an opportunity to give back by offering expertise to emerging designers and creatives.

There are many different ways to cultivate a creative community. Seek out a mentor or other like-minded peers. Try reading trade publications to gain a better understanding of the news and important issues in your creative field. Attend creative events either in person or virtually. Better still is to take a more active role in building a creative community through opportunities like joining a professional organization, attending a conference, or volunteering at a creative event. Creative community events such as workshops or lectures can provide inspiration, new skills, and a venue to share and celebrate work. Participating in these kinds of events may even create a path to creative leadership; experience may lead to an invitation to join a creative organization's board, promoting the organization's mission to reach its goal.

As the capacities of digital communities continue to evolve, there are plenty of ways to connect to communities online and remotely. This makes it easier for everyone to find an inspiring creative community, regardless of location or the ability and resources to attend in-person events, which sometimes have large price tags attached.

Nurture Existing Creative Community

Academic Mentors or Instructors

Everyone has a creative community, no matter the career phase. It's just a question of identifying it, connecting to it, and nurturing the relationships. How can you identify who is already in your creative network? An academic community is a good place to start. School instructors can be a great resource and source of connection. This connection with instructors can be developed into a meaningful community by attending office hours, asking for career advice, and taking part in extracurricular activities. If you're out of school, consider getting back in touch with former instructors, telling them about what you remember from their courses and how it shaped your work. Faculty members can be great resources because they may have suggestions for opportunities such as internships, conferences, and jobs. They may also be able to put you in touch with other program alumni.

Professional Supervisors or Bosses

The workplace can also be a great place to build a creative community. Colleagues and supervisors can double as creative community members. While not all managers have the time, it's worth inviting a boss or supervisor to coffee or lunch to chat with them about their career journey. It's also possible to learn through observation. Watch how supervisors interact with clients and manage difficult situations. Take note of what works well and consider how you might implement these strategies in your own practice. Observing how others interact and successfully use strong communication skills can offer important insights into problem-solving strategies and teamwork approaches. Complimenting a supervisor on their job well done can be a great way to strengthen your relationship with them and solidify their place in your creative community.

Colleagues

You can find mentors of all kinds throughout your organization, and you may be surprised to find that sometimes the best mentors come from a department or background that is completely unrelated to the creative field. The best way to develop these types of mentorships is to let them happen organically and to be open to scenarios that allow you to mingle with colleagues in other departments. This could mean participating in virtual or in-person events or inviting an acquaintance to coffee or lunch to get to know them better. Additionally, consider connecting with peers who are in your field but have a bit more experience or different experience than yours. Even just a year or two more experience can provide valuable insights and also, perhaps, a more relatable perspective than someone who is far more senior. The more you put yourself out there, the more likely you are to build relationships that will grow into fruitful creative connections and, if you are lucky, perhaps even great friendships.

Classmates

Classmates and peers serve as another important piece of a creative community. Shared experiences and challenges can produce an important sense of camaraderie. And it's always great to share successes and failures with someone who really "gets it." Upon graduation, maintain those relationships by setting up a peer feedback group to talk about professional experiences and creative ideas. Classmates can emerge as key collaborators through job referrals, collaborative projects, and other means.

Connecting with Friends

Design has many related creative fields, and it's great to branch out and connect with creatives from adjacent industries. For instance, if you work in advertising, try to meet more illustrators and motion designers to expand your horizons about the professional landscape of creative work and gain insights into the fields that often overlap with your area.

Grow a Creative Community

Growing a creative community takes more initiative than nurturing an existing community. It requires seeking out and cultivating new professional relationships. This may involve joining an existing professional group in your area or an online community, starting a brand-new community, or sharing work and knowledge to connect with peers. It can be overwhelming to try all these things at once, so start with just one. If it's not working, try something else. While growing a creative community can feel like a daunting task, it's worth the struggle. A creative community can help you feel more connected to your creativity and your industry. It can also help you build lasting professional and personal relationships.

Join a Local Professional Group

There are many established creative communities that welcome emerging professionals. The following list is a sample of professional groups where creatives can connect with others in their field. All these groups are national organizations (and some have a global reach) with regional arms throughout the United States.

American Advertising Federation (AAF) is a national organization that supports all disciplines in the field of advertising through local advertising clubs, college chapters, awards, and other activities.

AIGA, the professional association for design, extends its network to professional designers, students, educators, and design enthusiasts. It advocates professional standards in design, sponsors new research, and hosts events and exhibitions.

The **Public Relations Society of America** (PRSA) serves communication professionals and advocates for industry excellence and ethical conduct.

The **Society of Illustrators** promotes the art of illustration through exhibitions, lectures, and education.

Other Creative Organizations

The **Graphic Artists Guild** helps graphic artists and designers build successful careers through skill building, advice, and support.

Ladies Wine and Design is a global community created to support women and non-binary people in creative industries where they are underrepresented in leadership roles.

CreativeMornings sponsors free monthly gatherings featuring a talk by a creative professional. Though these events happen in cities across the globe, CreativeMornings expands its reach with CreativeGuild, a paid membership community where professionals can connect in an online space.

Toast Masters is not specific to creative industries but is an international organization that teaches public speaking through a worldwide network of clubs focused on helping people become more confident in public speaking and leadership roles.

Join an Online Community

There are countless online communities that offer meaningful connection with peers. Participating in an online community can be either active or passive depending on the structure and platform. For instance, many creative professionals use the Slack platform to keep connected both at work and in creative communities. For example, DevChat, "a very friendly group of software developers who come together to solve problems and learn," uses Slack to facilitate community.[2] This platform facilitates subject-specific virtual chat rooms as well as private messaging and file sharing features. Facebook, which allows private and moderated groups for specialized topics, can also cultivate online community. Other platforms, like Patreon and Twitch, which offer paid access to content, can also generate online communities. Sometimes these platforms facilitate community while in other cases, it's more of a one-way transmission of information whereby audiences learn and get access to new content from a presenter. Many online communities are facilitated through proprietary software platforms where participants can engage with each other in a more controlled platform.

A couple of examples of online membership communities include Rising Tide Society and Flourish. Rising Tide Society is a community of creative entrepreneurs founded by Honeybook, a project management and invoicing software developed for service-based small business owners. This can be a great resource for freelance professionals looking to find other self-employed creative professionals. Flourish is a membership platform for artists and designers looking to grow their surface design artwork and develop skills in creative entrepreneurship. Much like a professional organization, both of these online communities charge a monthly membership fee for access, and they both offer additional resources such as virtual events, educational content, and unique ways to share and connect within the given community.

Consider costs and terms as you seek out community. Some communities offer exclusive content, learning material, and unique collaboration in exchange for a one-time or recurring membership fee. While this can be a worthwhile expense, online communities don't always have to cost money. There are many free communities to be found online, and remember that it's always an option to start your own forum or community on an open access platform.

Start Your Own Community

To connect with like-minded creatives, it's sometimes most productive to build a new community group. After freelance graphic designer Christy Batta developed a handmade design for Amina Ahmad's Handmade Habitat candles, the two hit it off and starting meeting up regularly to create hand lettering projects. This designer/client relationship evolved into a creative friendship, and the two expanded their group by founding the Unofficial Hand Lettering Society of Silver Spring (Maryland). Today the group hosts monthly doodle sessions and workshop events. The focus isn't on professional networking—it's about connecting, creating, and trying something new. The example of Batta and Ahmad shows that there are many different paths to finding your people.[3]

Learn Something New

Learning a new skill such as coding, letterpress, or bookkeeping software is a great way to stay inspired or improve as a creative professional. Online and in-person courses are also a good route to meet other creative professionals and build your creative community. Some places to look for in-person courses include community makerspaces, continuing education programs at a local high school or community college, or even a local public library. If local resources aren't available, there are tons of online learning resources. Some online courses are just about skill acquisition, while others have built-in networks. For instance, many designers are tapped into Skillshare.com, where anyone can teach their skills to the community through project-based video lessons. Students can share their progress and final projects directly on the platform and get feedback and encouragement from others in the course. Other online learning platforms include LinkedIn Learning, Masterclass, and Creative Live, just to name a few. Sometimes it helps to join an online course with a friend or colleague to build accountability. It can also be a great opportunity to nurture the relationship offline by discussing projects and exchanging feedback to further learning and foster deeper connections.

Share Your Work

Though you may think of social media as a tool to connect with friends and family, leverage your familiarity with different apps to connect with other creative professionals. This may require thinking about the platform in a different way and taking more care in the material that you post and the professional identity you present, but by sharing creative work and process, social media can become a tool for building lasting relationships and growing a creative community.

Design challenges are a great way to start building a network. For example, during Inktober, a multiplatform event that happens every October, illustrators and designers from across the globe post an ink drawing every day of the month. By using hashtags and posting regularly, creatives can connect with others from around the world who share their interests. To find events like this, it helps to follow professional organizations and well-known creative professionals. Try following field-specific hashtags and topics to find challenges or conversations on social media.

Some social media platforms that are popular for creative professionals include Instagram and LinkedIn. Both of these work well for showcasing visual work. Additionally, Facebook and Twitter are commonly used by creative professionals. Other platforms to consider for connecting with creative professionals include Behance and Dribbble. Behance is an online portfolio platform designed for creative networking and showcasing visual work. Dribbble is a self-promotion and social media platform for designers and creatives. Members need to be invited to share work and the platform offers jobs, recruiting, and community. Other ways to share your work include participating in portfolio review events or presenting at local events or conferences—opportunities you might learn about through social media.

Share Your Skills

As your career develops, it's great to give back to the creative community by sharing your skills. This can take the form of mentorship and teaching, or even hosting workplace events such as lunch-and-learns in which colleagues give short presentations on their areas of expertise. This can be a good opportunity to work with your creative team to share new skills to improve creativity or workflow.

For example, Antoinette Carroll, the president and CEO of the non-profit organization Creative Reaction Lab, works on and off the clock to build diverse design communities. In her day job she works to "educate, train, and challenge Black and Latinx youth to become leaders designing healthy and racially equitable communities."[4] Outside of her job, she volunteers, mentors, and advocates for the design industry. For designers and creative professionals looking to build community by sharing skills and resources, Carroll suggests looking in your own backyard and identifying the challenges faced by local communities.[5]

Make-a-thon events are a great way to connect with other creative professionals and give back to your local community. A make-a-thon event combines the concept of making with a marathon by providing the structure for a team-based creative project to be completed in a predefined amount of time. Generally, the collaborative project also has some predefined objectives to help keep makers on task for their allotted time frame.

Make a Mark is a twelve-hour design and development make-a-thon benefitting local humanitarian causes. The purpose, as founder Sarah Obenauer describes it, is to provide beautiful design and technology to non-profits to help them share their stories. But there is another more human ambition too: "We are sharing experiences and spreading hope to one another. We are saying a small thank-you to those in our society that work tirelessly. We are building empathy in a world that needs it."[6]

CASE STUDY: MAKE A MARK: BUILDING COMMUNITY BY GIVING BACK

Sometimes a creative team is brought together for a limited amount of time. In this case study, learn how creative professionals are giving back to their communities.

Project
"Eyes Up" Campaign

Client
Second Life Tennessee

Creative Team
Jen Rezac, Deanna Kobet, Evie McNeese, Sarah Olivo were brought together as a team as part of the 2018 Make a Mark project.

Duration
2018
Like all Make a Mark project timelines, there is a one-hour planning meeting for the creative team and non-profit to meet up and exchange details about the project. On the day of the make-a-thon, the creative team works from 8:00 a.m. to 8:00 p.m. to complete the project.

Description
Each team member applied for the make-a-thon in advance and the Mark a Mark organizers put together teams and assigned them to clients based on the skills required for the project. In this case, the creative team was paired with the client, Second Life Tennessee, a Chattanooga-based non-profit organization whose mission is to end human sex trafficking in Southeast Tennessee.

   Second Life Tennessee wanted to build a brand identity and awareness campaign aimed at residents of Tennessee. The purpose was to highlight the national human trafficking hotlines and point out signs of human trafficking to watch out for in the community.

Process

In just twelve hours, the design team came up with a concept called "Eyes Up," which asked viewers to stay vigilant and take responsibility by reporting concerning activity in their local area. As the team stated in their presentation, "Victims of human trafficking are instructed to keep their eyes on the ground at all times. It's our responsibility to keep our eyes up."[7] The team developed a logo for the "Eyes Up" campaign along with posters, car stickers, and rack cards.

FIGURE 5.1 Make a Mark creative teams hard at work.

Make a Mark brings creative communities together to do good for their communities. Here you can see that even though they probably just met recently, these teams are working hard for their local non-profits to provide them with meaningful designs and content.

FIGURE 5.2 "Eyes Up" poster.

In twelve hours, the "Eyes Up" campaign was developed for the non-profit Second Life Tennessee.

FIGURE 5.3 "Eyes Up" stickers.

Each team created assets that would help the client. In this case, posters, stickers, and rack cards were most effective for the client to promote their message and raise awareness of their cause to local audiences.

FIGURE 5.4 "Eyes Up" rack cards.

The creative team worked together to develop creative copy, brand design, and page layout. Their combined skills and willingness to lean on each other for support helped bring the project together into one cohesive campaign with clear and consistent visual and written messaging.

Outcome

Second Life Tennessee program director Frances Warner said, "The final design was so much better than anything we could have imagined. We changed our entire vision and created an entire awareness campaign that we can share statewide with our partners."[8]

This creative work had an immediate positive impact on a social cause, and it also had positive outcomes for the designers involved in creating the campaign. Participant Sarah Olivo joined Make a Mark Chattanooga because she was new to the area and looking to connect with a creative community. Her advice to emerging designers is, "Don't shy away from opportunities because you look at them as 'networking' events. Think of them more as possibilities to extend your wheelhouse, home in on your own skills, share your knowledge and learn from others around you. Look into local lectures, buy a museum membership, or take a class. From those experiences, other opportunities will arise that are in line with your own path."[9] Olivo created an awareness campaign for Second Life Tennessee and can feel good about contributing to a humanitarian cause.

Questions for Thought

Do you feel prepared to contribute to a make-a-thon project?
What specialized creative skills would you bring to a team?
How do you build community in your personal life?
Are there skills you can adapt from your personal community network to help you with building a creative community?

FIGURE 5.5 "Eyes Up" client presentation.

At the end of each Make a Mark event, the creative team present their final concepts to the clients and celebrate together. Oftentimes the non-profits can't afford creative services and are blown away by the generosity and skill showcased in the work.

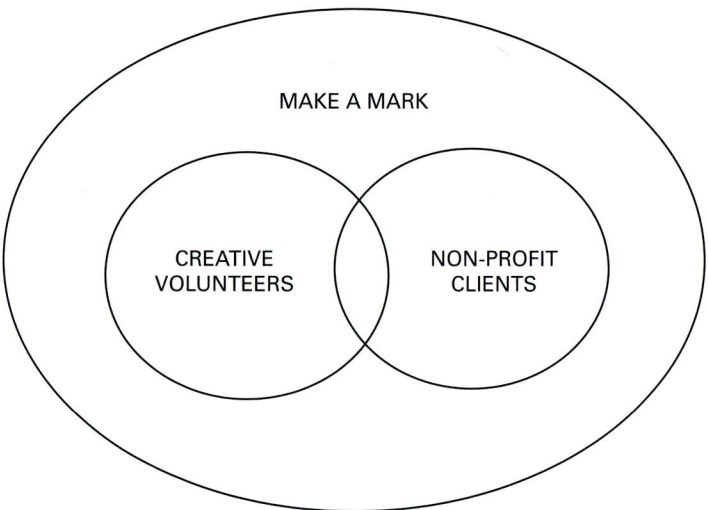

FIGURE 5.6 Team structure diagram.

Every Make a Mark project and client relationship is different because the teams are developed for one specific project and are brought together for a very short amount of time. The team structure is fairly simple in that everyone comes together through Make a Mark and creative teams of about three to five people collaborate with one non-profit client. The complexity comes with the limited time frame to complete the project and lack of a relationship between the team members. This is also the benefit of the event, because every team member has to quickly build trust and develop a strategy under pressure. This is a great experience for anyone interested in pushing their creative boundaries and building collaborative skills.

Embrace Mentorship

No matter the career stage, creative professionals benefit from mentorship. A good mentor can help guide your career toward a path of success. A mentor can be any experienced professional who you trust and who is willing to advise you on your career. Creative professionals should take care to find mentors who are inspiring and who are willing to give their time. These are the types of role models that understand the value mentorship adds to both the creative community and the profession.

Working for a strong female leader made a huge impact on Rose Newton's professional trajectory. Early in her career as a designer, she worked in a large corporate environment where she was responsible for creating internal education materials and executive presentation slides. When Newton was a junior team member, her boss would bring her to meetings where Newton didn't feel like she belonged. Newton's boss would even ask her to speak up and voice her opinions to the upper management team members. This told Newton that she was there for a reason and her opinions mattered. "I realized when my boss brought me to executive meetings that she wanted me to share in front of everyone."[10] Newton reflects that had she not received that exposure early in her career, "I don't think I would be where I am today."[11] Where is Newton today? She serves as a UX design manager at Google.

To pay forward the mentorship that was transformative for her own career, Newton has served on the AIGA Women Lead Steering Committee. By giving her time to this initiative, which is committed to empowering women in design, she's had an impact at a national level, helping women designers in the United States grow into leadership roles. Newton also provides mentorship to the women in her own company, borrowing strategies that she learned from her own mentor. She observes that one of the most common issues women face is that their ideas don't get heard or others take credit for their work. Newton tries to remedy this by giving women a voice and opportunities. "I always tell women stand your ground, fight for what you think is right, and stand up for yourself, and then keep being persistent about it."[12] Just as important as Newton's advice is the fact that her colleagues know she supports them and that they're not in it alone. By supporting the individuals on her team through involved mentorship, Newton is elevating the collective impact and abilities of her entire creative team.

Formal Mentorship Programs

There are numerous ways and places to find a mentor, and one option is to look for formal mentorship programs. For example, many corporations have formal mentorship programs that nurture talented emerging professionals. These structured programs provide early career professionals with access to senior-level people in their company, and help to bridge the gap in communication with peers in other departments. Additionally, some companies offer specific initiatives focused on promoting women's leadership or diversity, equity, and inclusion for creatives of color.

For example, AIG Insurance offers Employee Resource Groups that bring together employees with a shared identity such as Black Professionals & Allies, LGBTQ+ & Allies, Veterans, Young Professionals, and Working Families, to name a few.[13] AIG Insurance in-house designer Thomas Harris joined the LGBTQ+ and the Young Professionals groups to connect with like-minded peers, grow his community, and access professional development opportunities. "When I first started at AIG, I had to speak at an important meeting, and I wasn't happy with my performance," he remembers. "But I joined the Young Professionals group and worked on it. I've even hosted two community events for the group and my public speaking is noticeably improved because of that experience."[14] In the early stages of a career, it is important to break out of your comfort zone and learn how to communicate with other members of your organization. As a member of a creative team, this experience will help you to better understand the full scope of the company, get a sense of the company culture, and become a valuable member of the company community.

Other formal mentorship programs exist in university settings and through professional organizations. For instance, many colleges and universities pair senior-level students with incoming students for peer-to-peer mentorship. Others offer alumni mentorship programs for those who choose to take advantage of the resource. There are even some schools that provide mentorship opportunities with industry professionals or organizations.

Professional organizations often have formal mentorship programs for emerging professionals. These programs are designed to help educate future practitioners in the field. For instance, the American Advertising Federation offers a mentorship program; all members of the organization are eligible to participate as either mentors or mentees. While it's not essential to participate in a formal mentorship program to build community, it's worth exploring the available options to see if there's one that might be a good fit.

Quality Connection

Kathleen Shannon and Emily Thompson understand the importance of community. As the founders of *Being Boss*, a podcast aimed at creative entrepreneurs, they spent five years working together to build a strong network of like-minded individuals and figuring out how to build lasting connections.

The two agree that a building a strong community isn't about having thousands and thousands of followers online. Rather, it's often those more intimate connections that can really add value to your life and career. Thompson emphasizes the importance of being vulnerable and open to connection. "Talking about your credentials is not vulnerability, that's not a real connection," she says. "Showing up and giving a bit of yourself and asking really great questions and listening when the other person talks and telling about your dreams and aspirations … it's not the normal networking advice, but I find it's more beneficial and rewarding and creates deeper connections. I don't think you can run a business and make money (or at least I can't and feel good about it) without these deeper connections."[15] Like growing a garden, you can cultivate a creative network that, with the right care and attention, will thrive: "From meeting new people to sustaining long-term relationships, making and keeping friends is a habit you have to practice and nurture."[16]

Interview: Kathleen Shannon, Co-author of *Being Boss*[17]

How has your creative community impacted your creative life?

Shannon My creative community has offered support in so many ways—we share insights on systems, marketing methods, project workflow, and time management tips. Plus, we support each other not only as cheerleaders but as creative collaborators—we're often referring each other and even hiring each other on client work or our own projects.

What tips can you offer on how to cultivate a creative community?

Shannon   The beauty of the internet is that you can create real and meaningful relationships with like-minded creatives who live all over the world—but nothing beats meeting someone face to face. My best recommendation is to invest in attending conferences and retreats to gather with other creatives. You might meet a handful of people that you really connect with and from there you have to get intentional about setting a regular date and time to meet up—whether that's a weekly mastermind chat over video-conferencing software or a monthly phone call.

Also, when it comes to connecting with other creatives, don't think about shallow networking where you're exchanging business cards and polished elevator pitches. Instead think about exchanging meaningful stories and valuable insights so that you can create and nurture real relationships.

What tips do you have for those who feel shy about building new relationships?

Shannon   I've found that most creative entrepreneurs identify as introverts, so if you're feeling shy, you're not alone! I would recommend finding an online group of like-minded people—you can develop real and meaningful relationships with folks from the safety of your own home. Also, creatives live everywhere and it's easier than ever to find creative clubs, events, and people by first searching online or on social media for your tribe. It will definitely take a little courage to meet up with people, especially if you're an introvert, so one thing I recommend is having a list of questions you can ask. Try going beyond "what do you do for a living?" and ask folks what book or podcast they're loving, or what they've learned recently.

What value do you see in online communities versus in-person communities?

Shannon   Online communities are amazing for meeting a lot of people in a quick amount of time. When you're hooked into an online network you can get quick feedback and responses to almost any question you have. We used to say "IRL," which stands for "in real life" when referring to how you know someone—but the funny thing is that these days online *is* real! Even so, nothing compares to meeting someone in person. While online communities will help you build your network far and wide, in-person communities will feed your humanity! With in-person communities you can develop meaningful friendships and more inherent trust than you do from behind your laptop.

What advice do you have for someone looking to grow a creative community either online or in-person?

Shannon My best advice is to know that a community isn't a marketplace—a community is about cultivating generous and real conversations. It's also a really good idea to start small so you can establish tone, boundaries, and trust with an inner circle that can hold the community to the standards you set as you begin to grow.

Community Lasts a Career

Building a creative community is important for staying inspired throughout a creative career. Whether you find your niche in a local professional organization, an online space with people from all over the globe, or even start something new with a small group of like-minded peers, being part of a creative community will be meaningful. In fact, oftentimes it can be one of the most rewarding aspects of a creative career! While it's important to focus on developing professional skills, take time to foster those deeper connections in your community. Cultivate long-lasting relationships by seeking and offering support. The members of your creative community are the people that will be there to help you through difficult professional transitions and to celebrate your successes in the creative space.

EXERCISE: FINDING A CREATIVE MENTOR

Mentorship is possible inside and outside of the workplace. This exercise invites you to find a mentor outside of work.

Attending a professional organization event such as a mixer, workshop, lecture, or conference in your home city is great way to meet other professionals who might become great mentors. Don't forget to leverage the networks you already belong to. You can utilize social networking sites such as LinkedIn and Twitter, or you can try more traditional networks such as your alumni association. Additionally, reach out to professionals at various levels in their career. For instance, if you are fresh out of college, someone with two years of experience might be able to provide more insight into the current job market than a professional with twenty years of experience. On the flip side, someone who is at the height of their career can give you a unique understanding of what it takes to sustain a long-term creative career.

After identifying a possible mentor, it's best to build the relationship organically. (In other words, don't ask them to be your mentor! This can be a lot of pressure!) Focus on establishing the connection. For instance, you could take your colleague out for a coffee in exchange for picking their brain about how they advanced their career. Follow up with a quick thank-you email, and update them periodically (no more than quarterly) on what you've been creating at work. By staying connected, you have found yourself a mentor that you can reach out to when you need them to weigh in on your next big career move.

However, if they're not replying, that might mean they're not able to commit to developing the relationship. That's okay too! You've taken the first step in developing your creative community, and that willingness to be vulnerable deserves a pat on the back . . . now keep on connecting!

Not sure how to find a mentor? Try one of these ideas to get out of your comfort zone.

Prompt 1: Leverage social media

Tweet (or tag or do whatever it is they do on your preferred social media platform) five designers you admire and would like to have as a mentor. Try finding strategies to get them to tweet back and keep the conversation going. Remember, your social media presence is a public representation of you, so keep the conversation polite and respectful! If you reach three tweets back from the designer, follow up with an email; keep it short and to the point and ask one poignant question. If they respond, make sure to send a thank-you email that describes how their advice was useful for you in your career.

Prompt 2: Interview

As discussed in previous chapters, consider reaching out to a design professional in your local area and conducting an interview about their creative career path. Use the content from your interview to design a visually compelling display of the interview, such as a poster, motion graphic, or book. Don't forget to share your outcome with your interviewee and get permission to publish it on your portfolio. You can even politely ask for design feedback if their schedule allows.

Prompt 3: Buy them a coffee

Mentorship is not always a formal process. It can be as simple as offering to buy a peer a coffee and chatting about your work and professional goals. Nurturing these relationships will be rewarding and invigorating. Don't feel like you have to ask permission to consider someone a mentor, just ask to buy them a coffee and go from there!

Prompt 4: Become a mentor

Give back to your community and create professional karma by mentoring an aspiring designer. Help them by critiquing their work, teaching them a new skill, or assisting them with a school project. (Hint: If you are still a college student, consider inviting art students from a local high school to your class or ask if an area high school would like a student volunteer to talk to the students about college. Provide the students you speak with tips and advice based on your experiences as a college student.)

CONCLUSION

Now that you've read this book, you're fully equipped to emerge and thrive in the creative space. As parting advice, here are some tips for emerging creative professionals that you can start working on today, regardless of whether or not you're working on a team just yet.

JUNIOR ESPINOZA'S TIPS FOR EMERGING DESIGNERS[1]

Junior Espinoza understands the competitive landscape of the design field and works hard to set himself apart through a meticulous curation and presentation of his design portfolio. Beginning his work as a graphic design professional in 2014, he's since had a range of experiences working both in-house and on the agency side. Here is his advice for emerging designers:

1. **Figure Out What You Want.** This is a not-to-be-missed question, because if you don't know what you want, you won't know where to start and you can feel vulnerable and lost. Make a conscious decision and commit 100 percent to what interests you.

2. **Find a Mentor, Colleague, or Even a Former Professor Who You Can Turn To.** It's important for us to keep in touch with our mentors because they can provide the proper guidance and support when needed.

3. **Improve Your Skills Every Day.** I suggest that designers stay current on software like Illustrator, Photoshop, and InDesign, because they serve as tools to improve skills while having fun being creative. If you don't feel like you're having fun, then this career might not be for you.

4. **Start Designing.** If you wait for the right time or the right amount of knowledge before starting a project, it's never going to happen. Being a perfectionist doesn't get you anywhere. Try to find a brief so you can start practicing. You can even make your own brief to get your creative juices flowing. Play around with your sketch ideas and dig deeper into infinite possibilities of creativity.

5. **Get Your Portfolio Ready ASAP and Know Your Strengths.** A portfolio is critical for both non-experienced and experienced designers. It is simply the embodiment of who we are. And remember that your portfolio will always evolve, so do not get emotionally attached to it. The projects will come and go as time passes. Focus on developing the projects you're working on so you can seize an opportunity and hit the ground running. Create your own projects and determine which ones are worthy for your portfolio.

6. **On Rejection.** I'm a deaf designer, and it was a huge blessing for me to find a job because not many job seekers (deaf or hearing) can find their dream job after college. My goal is to inspire and show everyone that you can never give up. Embrace rejection and grow tough skin. I've faced rejection several times, but I persisted in honing my skills and finding a job. Write down goals and don't stop until you reach them.

7. **Work Smarter and Keep Learning.** If you want to work in a fast-paced environment, focus on working smarter and not harder. Don't spend hours trying to perfect your work. Find tutorials online such as workflow, software shortcuts, techniques, etc. And don't ever be afraid to ask questions if you feel stuck. Good ideas are never going to happen if I do *not* ask questions. This is only going to help you become an efficient designer. Period.

Final Thoughts: This journey has been so incredible because I've overcome a lot of obstacles in my life and didn't allow my deafness to become a hindrance in my career. And remember that you're not alone in this. Just have fun and be creative!

Now that you have some actionable steps for what you can work on today to land a job on a team tomorrow, let's recap what you now know about creative teams.

First, it's essential to understand what makes a successful creative team. When working on a creative team, it's important to cultivate a sense of creative safety and develop clear communication and expectations. Additionally, a proactive approach to improving diversity, equity, and inclusion will result in greater team success. As a team member, it's vital to demonstrate a commitment to the team's success through strong communication, reliability, and initiative. By understanding and writing down your own values, you can start to envision the ideal creative team for your lifestyle, goals, and work habits.

There are three primary types of teams for creative professionals: agency, in-house, and freelance. Agency work is direct-to-client and comes in all shapes and sizes, and offers numerous teamwork structures. There's likely an agency model for your preferred teamwork style. While the creative output is much like an agency team, in-house work provides unique opportunities and challenges; the latter include negative perceptions from other creatives and lack of understanding from other arms of the organization, yet you also get to have a long-term meaningful impact on the development of a brand that isn't common on any other type of creative team. As a freelancer, working for yourself can be rewarding so long as the independence suits you. You need to be able to be accountable for yourself, have a strong network to field new clients, and develop a strong reputation to keep existing clients coming back time and again to work with you.

Last, it's imperative to build a creative community as an extension of your creative team. Nurturing these relationships will help you feel more connected, inspired, and can bring lasting friendships that endure throughout your career.

As mentioned at the beginning of this book, many of the professionals interviewed have moved on to new roles and changed positions within their careers. Even though jobs change and professionals evolve, the collaborative skills described in this book are always useful. No matter the position, understanding how to work on a team is essential, because teamwork and collaboration are fundamental to creative work.

As you develop as a creative professional, this toolkit will help you on your journey through your creative career and set you on a path to thrive in the creative space.

ACKNOWLEDGMENTS

I want to say a special thank-you to Maggie Taft for her help with editing and coaching me through the writing process. I couldn't have finished this project without her thoughtful feedback and support.

Thank you to everyone who took part in an interview with me for this project. Talking with industry professionals and educators was an invaluable part of my research for this project, and I appreciate all the time and energy that was generally given to help me in this endeavor.

Interview Contributors

Aldo Arias
Christy Batta
Libby Bawcombe
Michael Bierut
Liz Blazer
Vanessa Carney
Antionette Carroll
Kristen Curtis
Aaron Davis
Vanessa Dewey
Tom Drymalski
Junior Espinoza
Dan Ferguson
Joah Gerstenberg
Mitch Goldstein
Helen Greene
Brooke Harmon
Thomas Harris
Luke Hayman
Paul Jarvis
Natasha Jen

Allyson Lack
Ellen Lupton
Evan Maeda
Angelica McKinley
Daniel McLemore
Gwendolyn Mumford
Veda Nagpurkar
Daniel Newman
Rose Newton
Sarah Obenauer
Devin O'Bryan
Sarah Olivio
Emma Sexton
Kathleen Shannon
Steve Simpson
Maggie Sterner
Ramona Todoca
Frances Warner

Image credits

Figures 1.1–1.5: Courtesy of Pentagram
Figure 2.5: Courtesy of Anthony Fomin
Figure 2.6: The New Yorker cover image with coverlines June 3, 2013 page 1 by Marcellus Hall, The New Yorker © Condé Nast
Figure 2.8: Photograph by Stephen Rees
Figure 2.9: Courtesy of Tom Drymalski
Figure 3.1 and 3.2: Courtesy of Emma Sexton, © Inside Out Awards
Figure 3.3: Courtesy of Neil Bedford, Making Pictures
Figure 4.1: Courtesy of Steve Simpson
Figures 4.2–4.4: Courtesy of Steve Simpson and Oskar Perrson, Jameson Irish Whiskey
Figure 5.1: Courtesy of Sarah Obenauer, Make a Mark
Figures 5.2–5.4: Courtesy of Make a Mark
Figure 5.5: Courtesy of Sarah Obenauer, Make a Mark

FURTHER READING

Chapter 1

Intercultural Collaboration by Design: Drawing from Differences, Distances, and Disciplines Through Visual Thinking by Denielle J. Emans and Kelly M. Murdoch-Kitt is a handbook developed to help work, learn, and teach across cultures. It offers over thirty hands-on activities to help teams achieve success.

The book *Being Boss: Take Control of Your Work and Live Life on Your Own Terms* by Kathleen Shannon and Emily Thompson has several exercises geared towards creative entrepreneurs including one to help define your core values. This will be particularly useful if you'd like to dive deeper into defining your own core values.

Diversity, Equity, and Inclusion in Design:
Field Guide: Equity Centered Community Design by Creative Reaction Lab and Antoinette Carroll

Black, Brown + Latinx Design Educators: Conversations on Design and Race by Kelly Walters

Extra Bold: A Feminist, Inclusive, Anti-racist, Nonbinary Field Guide for Graphic Designers by Ellen Lupton, Jennifer Tobias, Josh Halstead, Leslie Xia, Kaleena Sales, Farah Kafei, and Valentina Vergara

Chapter 2

To learn more about creative professionals and different opportunities for working in design, read *The AIGA Guide to Careers in Graphic & Communication Design* by Juliette Cezzar. This book offers many insightful interviews with creative professionals and can help with structuring your own interview questions.

Chapter 3

Cella is a leading management consultancy for in-house agencies and creative teams based in the United States. Since 2010, they have published annual 'In-House Creative Industry

Reports' which highlight trends and forecast the future of the in-house creative industry. Reports are available for free online at https://www.cellaconsulting.com/tools-and-resources/industry-benchmarking/.

Chapter 4

Here are some books that can help with the more detailed aspects of setting up a freelance practice:

- *Art, Inc.: The Essential Guide for Building Your Career as an Artist* by Lisa Congdon (San Francisco: Chronicle Books, 2014).
- *The Freelance Way: Best Business Practices, Tools & Strategies for Freelancers* by Robert Vlach (Brno: Jan Melvin Publishing, 2019).
- *How to Be a Graphic Designer without Losing Your Soul* (New Expanded Edition) by Adrian Shaughnessy (New York: Princeton Architectural Press, 2012).
- *Working for Yourself: Law & Taxes for Independent Contractors, Freelancers & Gig Workers of All Types* by Stephen Fishman J.D. (Berkeley, California: Nolo, 2019).

While these books offer a good starting point, there are many ways to shape a freelance career. To define the right path, it's important to consider goals, strengths, and work habits.

If you want to learn more about creating a great first impression as a freelancer read *Captivate: The Science of Succeeding with People* by Vanessa Van Edwards, a behavior investigator and creator of People School. The book provides many exercises and tools to help readers "succeed with people."

Chapter 5

If you're wondering about why community is important to a creative career (or just to human existence in general) read *The Art of Gathering: How We Meet and Why It Matters* by Priva Parker. The book goes into detail about what makes gatherings of people effective and memorable and gives insights into how to make your own gatherings more impactful for everyone involved.

NOTES

1 SURVIVING THE CREATIVE SPACE

1. Michael Bierut, Email to author, November 2, 2017.
2. Aggie Toppins, "Can We Teach Graphic Design History Without the Cult of Hero Worship," *AIGA Eye on Design*, May 29, 2020, https://eyeondesign.aiga.org/can-we-teach-graphic-design-history-without-the-cult-of-hero-worship/.
3. *ibid/*.
4. Bill Bernbach, quoted in John McDonough and Karen Egolf, *The Advertising Age Encyclopedia of Advertising* (London: Routledge, 2015), 166.
5. Bill Bernbach, quoted in "Doyle Dane Bernbach," *Communication Arts*, accessed May 3, 2021, https://www.commarts.com/features/doyle-dane-bernbach.
6. "The Value of Design," DMI: Design Management Institute, accessed May 3, 2021, https://www.dmi.org/page/DesignValuc.
7. Debbie Yong, "The Design Value Index Shows What 'Design Thinking' is Worth," *Fortune*, August 30, 2017, http://fortune.com/2017/08/31/the-design-value-index-shows-what-design-thinking-is-worth/.
8. "Vanessa Dewey, Sr. Product Marketing Manager," Adobe Blog, accessed October 7, 2021, https://blog.adobe.com/en/authors/vanessa-dewey.html.
9. John Branch, "Snow Fall: The Avalanche at Tunnel Creek," *New York Times*, accessed February 24, 2022, https://www.nytimes.com/projects/2012/snow-fall/index.html#/?part=tunnel-creek.
10. Angelica McKinley, Phone interview with author, May 21, 2018.
11. "Van Leeuwen," Pentagram, accessed May 21, 2021, https://www.pentagram.com/work/van-leeuwen/story.
12. Dorothy Tan, "Pentagram's Colorful, Strikingly Minimal Packaging Boosts Ice Cream Sales," *Taxi*, July 21, 2017, https://designtaxi.com/news/394420/Pentagram-s-Colorful-Strikingly-Minimal-Packaging-Boosts-Ice-Cream-Sales/.
13. Meredith Davis, "Complex Problems," AIGA – Design Futures Research, accessed May 3, 2021, https://www.aiga.org/sites/default/files/2021-02/Complex%20Problems.pdf.
14. "Design Futures Research," AIGA, accessed May 3, 2021, https://www.aiga.org/resources/design-futures-research.

15 S. O'Dea, "Number of Smartphone Users Worldwide from 20216 to 2023," *Statista*, March 31, 2021, https://www.statista.com/statistics/330695/number-of-smartphone-users-worldwide/

16 Charles Duhigg, *Smarter Faster Better: The Transformative Power of Real Productivity* (Random House Books, 2017), 50–1.

17 Ramona Todoca, Phone interview with author, March 19, 2019.

18 Erik Larson, "New Research: Inclusive Decision Making Increases Performance of Diverse Global Companies," *Cloverpop*, September 19, 2017, https://www.cloverpop.com/blog/new-research-inclusive-decision-making-increases-performance-of-diverse-global-companies.

19 Creative Reaction Lab, "Field Guide: Equity Centered Community Design" [pamphlet], 2018, https://www.creativereactionlab.com/store/p/field-guide-equity-centered-community-design, 10–11.

20 Sarah Saska, "How to define diversity, equity, and inclusion," *Cultureamp*, accessed May 3, 2021, https://www.cultureamp.com/blog/how-to-define-diversity-equity-and-inclusion-at-work.

21 Kelly Walters *Black, Brown + Latinx Design Educators* (New York: Princeton Architectural Press, 2021), 174.

22 Juliet Bourke and Andrea Titus, "The Key to Inclusive Leadership," *Harvard Business Review*, March 6, 2020, https://hbr.org/2020/03/the-key-to-inclusive-leadership.

23 Denielle J. Emans and Kelly M. Murdoch-Kitt, *Intercultural Collaboration by Design: Drawing from Differences, Distances, and Disciplines Through Visual Thinking* (New York: Routledge, 2020), 16.

24 Tomas Chamorro-Premuzic, "Why Group Brainstorming is a Waste of Time," *Harvard Business Review*, March 25, 2015, https://hbr.org/2015/03/why-group-brainstorming-is-a-waste-of-time.

25 Ben Taylor, "Why Most Brainstorms Don't Work," *Dropbox: Work in Progress*, August 8, 2019, https://blog.dropbox.com/topics/work-culture/how-to-brainstorm.

26 IBM, "IBM Design Thinking Field Guide," accessed May 26, 2021, https://www-356.ibm.com/partnerworld/wps/static/watsonbuild/media/IBM%20Design%20Thinking%20Field%20Guide%20Watson%20Build%20v3.5_ac.pdf.

27 National Equity Project, "Developing Community Agreements," accessed June 3, 2021, https://www.nationalequityproject.org/tools/developing-community-agreements.

28 AIGA, the professional association for design encourages companies to offer paid internship opportunities. Furthermore, the AIGA Philadelphia chapter asks companies to take a "Paid Internship Pledge" to help end the exploitation and end inequities created by unpaid internships: https://philadelphia.aiga.org/unpaid-internship-pledge/. Additional information about internship guidelines in the United States can be found at US Department of Labor's website: https://www.dol.gov/sites/dolgov/files/WHD/legacy/files/whdfs71.pdf

29 Ellen Lupton, Phone interview with the author, May 24, 2018.

30 Denielle J. Emans and Kelly M. Murdoch-Kitt, *Intercultural Collaboration by Design: Drawing from Differences, Distances, and Disciplines Through Visual Thinking* (New York: Routledge, 2020), 19.

31 Harvey Deutschendorf, "Why Emotionally Intelligent People are More Successful," Fast Company, June 22, 2015, https://www.fastcompany.com/3047455/why-emotionally-intelligent-people-are-more-successful.

32 Antoinette Carroll, Phone interview with author, February 5, 2019.

33 Meredith Davis, "Introduction to Design Futures," AIGA – Design Futures, accessed May 16, 2021, https://www.aiga.org/sites/default/files/2021-02/introduction-to-design-futures.pdf.

34 Ellen Lupton, Phone interview with author, May 24, 2018.

35 Devin O'Bryan, "Emotional Intelligence: A Descent into the Maelstrom," LinkedIn Pulse, April 6, 2016, https://www.linkedin.com/pulse/emotional-intelligence-descent-maelstrom-devin-o-bryan/.

36 Meredith Davis, "Core Values Matter," AIGA – Design Futures, accessed May 16, 2021, https://www.aiga.org/sites/default/files/2021-02/Core%20Values%20Matter.pdf.

2 AGENCY TEAMS

1 Allyson Lack, "An Evening with Paula Scher," Introductory Remarks, AIGA Houston + Principle, Houston, Texas, February 1, 2018.

2 Allyson Lack, Interview with author, April 12, 2018.

3 "Top 10 Largest Advertising Agencies Worldwide 2020, Top Advertising Agencies Advertising Industry," BizVibe, accessed May 19, 2021, https://blog.bizvibe.com/blog/largest-advertising-agencies.

4 "The Best Organizational Structure of an Ad Agency," Cor, accessed May 19, 2021, https://projectcor.com/the-best-organizational-structure-of-an-ad-agency/.

5 Juliette Cezzar, *The AIGA Guide to Careers in Graphic and Communication Design* (New York: Bloomsbury Academic, 2017), 47.

6 *ibid*, 50.

7 *ibid*, 52.

8 *ibid*, 50.

9 *ibid*, 47.

10 Luke Hayman, Phone interview with author, March 1, 2018.

11 Michael Bierut, Email to author, November 2, 2017.

12 Natasha Jen, Phone interview with author, November 21, 2017.

13 *ibid*.

14 *ibid*.

15 *ibid*.

16 *ibid*.

17 Veda Nagpurkar and Brooke Harmon, Email interview with author, January 11, 2019.

18 Cezzar, 50.

19 Allyson Lack, Interview with author, April 12, 2018.

20 *ibid*.

21 Tom Drymalski, Interview with author, October 23, 2018.

22 *ibid.*

23 Cezzar, 52.

24 Tara Street, "Episode 56: Owning Your Creative Expertise," *Being Boss,* January 26, 2016, https://beingboss.club/podcast/podcast-episode-56-owning-your-creative-expertise-tara-street.

25 Cezzar, 50.

26 Helen Greene, Interview with author, February 21, 2018.

27 Liz Blazer, Phone interview with author, January 22, 2019.

28 *ibid.*

29 Helen Greene, Interview with author, February 21, 2018.

30 "Dallas Mavericks Commemorates Dirk Nowitzki's Retirement with AR Fan Engagement," Groove Jones, April 16, 2019, https://www.groovejones.com/dallas_mavericks_dirk_nowitzki_ar/.

31 Dan Ferguson, Email interview with author, October 30, 2018.

32 Natasha Jen, Phone interview with author, November 21, 2017.

33 Leeann Leahy, "The Future of Agency Models," *Forbes,* August 30, 2018, https://www.forbes.com/sites/forbesagencycouncil/2018/08/30/the-future-of-agency-models/?sh=1b4954904489.

3 IN-HOUSE TEAMS

1 Daniel McLemore, Interview with author, July 17, 2017.

2 The Boss Group, "2018 In-House Creative Industry Report," accessed May 26, 2021, https://insights.cellainc.com/hubfs/IHIR/2018/2018_ihcsir_report_by_boss_and_cella.pdf; The Boss Group, "2021 In-House Creative Industry Report," accessed May 26, 2021, https://www.cellainc.com/insights/in-house-industry-report/.

3 Bradley Johnson, "2019 was the Weakest Year for Agency Growth Since the Great Recession . . .," *AdAge,* May 11, 2020, https://adage.com/article/datacenter/2019-was-weakest-year-agency-growth-great-recession-bad-news-2020/2255381.

4 The Boss Group, "2018 In-House Creative Industry Report".

5 Emma Sexton, Skype interview with author, June 28, 2018.

6 *ibid.*

7 "Spotify Transports NYC Commuters to Mars with Immersive David Bowie Subway Takeover," Spotify, April 17, 2018, https://newsroom.spotify.com/2018-04-17/spotify-transports-nyc-commuters-to-mars-with-immersive-david-bowie-subway-takeover/.

8 Sarah Vizard, "How Spotify built its in-house creative team," *Marketing Week,* August 17, 2018, https://www.marketingweek.com/2018/08/17/spotify-in-house-creative-team/.

9 Beverly Bethge and William Faust, "Working as One: Creative Teams and Outside Agencies," *DMI Review* 20, no. 3 (September 2011), 19.

10 Emma Sexton, Skype interview with author, June 28, 2018.

11 "How in-house creative teams benefit from winning awards," Inside Out Awards, April 26, 2019, https://www.insideoutawards.com/awardnews/2019/4/26/how-in-house-creative-teams-benefit-from-winning-awards.

12 "Pentland Brands wins In-House Design award for Best Project," Pentland Brands, November 8, 2019, https://pentlandbrands.com/pentland-brands-wins-in-house-design-award-for-best-project/.

13 *ibid*.

14 Daniel McLemore, Interview with author, July 17, 2017.

15 *ibid*.

16 Angelica McKinley, Phone interview with author, May 21, 2018.

17 Ron Stodghill, "Harriet Tubman's Path to Freedom," *New York Times*, February 24, 2017, https://www.nytimes.com/interactive/2017/02/24/travel/underground-railroad-slavery-harriet-tubman-byway-maryland.html.

18 Angelica McKinley, Phone interview with author, May 21, 2018.

19 Libby Bawcombe and Daniel Newman, Skype interview with author, May 8, 2018.

20 Design at NPR, accessed April 26, 2021, https://npr.design.

21 Libby Bawcombe, "How to Interrupt: A quick guide for introverts and steamrollers," Design at NPR, July 19, 2017, https://npr.design/how-to-interrupt-a686eb7dedf1.

22 Veronica Erb, "How to Stop Steamrolling and Start Thinking Together," Design at NPR, July 19, 2017, https://npr.design/how-to-stop-steamrolling-and-start-thinking-together-a72ab3348ebc.

23 *ibid*.

24 Devin O'Bryan, Phone interview with author, April 13, 2017.

25 Mark Wilson, "IBM Invests $100 Million to Expand Design Business," Fast Company, March 27, 2014, https://www.fastcompany.com/3028271/ibm-invests-100-million-to-expand-design-business.

26 The Boss Group, "2021 In-House Creative Industry Report," 28–9.

27 The Boss Group, "2018 In-House Creative Industry Report".

28 Nida Abdullah, quoted in Walters, *Black, Brown + Latinx Design Educators*, 60.

29 *ibid*.

30 Gwendolyn Mumford and Thomas Harris, Interview with author, April 12, 2018.

4 FREELANCE TEAMS

1 Vanessa Carney, Phone interview with author, May 14, 2018.

2 *ibid*.

3 Paul Jarvis, Phone interview with author, April 12, 2018.

4 "The Future of Freelancing," Robert Half, March 13, 2018, https://www.roberthalf.com/blog/the-future-of-work/the-future-of-freelancing.

5 The Graphic Artists Guild, *Graphic Artists Guild Handbook*, 16th Edition (Cambridge, MA: The MIT Press, 2021).

6   See, for example: Jessica Hische, "The Dark Art of Pricing," accessed May 27, 2021, https://www.jessicahische.shop/product/the-dark-art-of-pricing; "Freelance Rates Explorer," HelloBonsai, accessed May 27, 2021, https://www.hellobonsai.com/freelance-rates; "Creative & Marketing," Robert Half, accessed May 27, 2021, https://www.roberthalf.com/salary-guide/creative-and-marketing.

7   The Editors, "It's Time for Graphic Design to Embrace the Radical Potential of Salary Transparency," *AIGA Eye on Design*, December 9, 2019, https://eyeondesign.aiga.org/its-time-for-graphic-design-to-embrace-the-radical-potential-of-salary-transparency-%F0%9F%92%B8/.

8   Steven Simpson, Skype interview with author, November 1, 2018.

9   *ibid.*

10 *ibid.*

11 An Xiao, "'Procrastinating' Your Way to Creative Success," *Hyperallergic*, April 24, 2012, https://hyperallergic.com/50227/procrastiworking-your-way-to-creative-success/.

12 Steven Simpson, Skype interview with author, November 1, 2018.

13 "Jameson LE Label," Steve Simpson, accessed April 27, 2021, https://stevesimpson.com/jameson-limited-edition-bottle.

14 Felicity Murray, "Jameson unveils Hello Dublin edition bottle," The Drinks Report, January 26, 2015, https://www.thedrinksreport.com/news/2015/15835-jameson-unveils-hello-dublin-edition-bottle.html/.

15 *ibid.*

16 *ibid.*

17 Aldo Arias and Kristen Curtis, Phone interview with author, July 3, 2018.

18 *ibid.*

19 *ibid.*

20 *ibid.*

21 Christy Batta, Phone interview with author, April 3, 2018.

22 *ibid.*

23 *ibid.*

24 Paul Jarvis, Phone interview with author, April 12, 2018.

25 Maggy Sterner, Phone interview with author, April 12, 2018.

26 *ibid.*

27 Christy Batta, Phone interview with author, April 3, 2018.

28 Paul Jarvis, *Company of One* (Boston: Houghton Mifflin Harcourt, 2019), xv.

29 Jarvis, *Company of One*, xv–xvi.

30 Vanessa Carney, Phone interview with author, May 14, 2018.

5 COMMUNITY AS AN EXTENSION OF CREATIVE TEAM

1   Sarah Obenauer, Email to author, February 1, 2019.

2   DevChat, accessed April 27, 2021, https://devchat.dev.

3. Jennifer Barrios, "When the Written Word Becomes Art One Letter at a Time," *The Washington Post*, December 26, 2018, https://www.washingtonpost.com/local/md-politics/when-the-written-word-becomes-art-one-letter-at-a-time/2018/12/26/59469b82-ff35-11e8-83c0-b06139e540e5_story.html?noredirect=on&utm_term=.fe379ca13cfe.

4. Creative Reaction Lab, "About," accessed May 30, 2021, https://www.creativereactionlab.com/about.

5. Antoinette Carroll, Phone interview with author, February 5, 2019.

6. Sarah Obenauer, Email to author, February 1, 2019.

7. Sarah Obenauer, "Second Life Tennessee: 2018 Chattanooga Make-a-Thon Case Study," December 14, 2018, https://medium.com/makeamark/second-life-tennessee-5e02bb97aa5a.

8. Frances Warner, Email to author, February 1, 2019.

9. Sarah Olivio, Email to author, April 25, 2019.

10. Rose Newton, Skype interview with author, November 3, 2017.

11. *ibid.*

12. *ibid.*

13. "Diversity, Equity, and Inclusion," AIG, accessed April 28, 2021, https://www.aig.com/about-us/diversity-and-inclusion.

14. Thomas Harris, Interview with author, April 12, 2018.

15. Emily Thompson, "Episode 200: Surprising Business Lessons," *Being Boss* [Podcast], October 30, 2018, 36:48, https://beingboss.club/podcast/surprising-business-lessons.

16. Emily Thompson and Kathleen Shannon, *Being Boss: Take Control of Your Work and Live Life on Your Own Terms* (Running Press, 2018), 188–9.

17. Kathleen Shannon, Email to author, November 14, 2018.

CONCLUSION

1. Junior Espinoza, Email to author, March 25, 2019.

INDEX

Note: Illustrations are indicated by the suffix '*ill.*' and figures by the suffix '*fig.*'

Abdullah, Professor Nidah 65
academic communities 94–5 *see also* students
account manager, role of 17, 31, 34
accountability 14, 18, 72
advertising 2–3, 24, 27, 36–8, 84–6, 96 *see also* agencies
agencies 10, 114 *see also* advertising; teams
    case study: Citi Bike: Collaborating on a multifaceted campaign 36–41, 38–40*ill.*
    definitions 26–8
    evolution of 45–7
    and freelancers 74
    and in-house teams 51, 53–4, 66
    as learning environments 85
    marketing 37
    role of 23–4
    structure 25*ill.*, 45–9
agents 76
agile processes 62, 63, 64
Ahmad, Amina 98
AIG Insurance 65–8, 107
AIGA (American Institute of Graphic Arts) 9, 96, 107
American Advertising Federation (AAF) 96, 108
animation 28, 43, 44–5
Arias, Aldo 84–6
art directors 17, 32, 34–5, 84–6
augmented reality 46
awards 54–9, 76–7

Batta, Christy 86–8, 98
Bawcombe, Libby 62
Behance online platform 76
Being Boss podcast 108
Benn, James 56
Bernbach, Bill 2–3
Bethge, Beverly 53–4
bias, personal 14
Bierut, Michael 2, 28
billing *see* fees
Black creatives 107
Blazer, Liz: *Animated Storytelling* 45
Braid Creative consultancy 42
brainstorming 15, 61
Branch, John: "Snow Fall: The Avalanche at Tunnel Creek" 4
branding 4–8, 29, 37, 42, 60, 65
    agencies 24, 27, 35–6
    in-house 69–70
briefs, creative 61
burnout 66–7
businesses 52–3, 56, 65, 68, 73

Canterbury brand 56, 57–8*ill.*, 59*fig.*
Carnegie Institute of Technology 18–19
Carney, Vanessa 89
Carroll, Antoinette 18–19, 99
Cezzar, Juliette: *The AIGA Guide to Careers in Graphic and Communication Design* 28
Citi Bike (Citibank) campaign 36–41, 38–40*ill.*
clients
    charging 45, 72–3

communication with 34–5, 42
direct-to-client working 73
internal 52, 61
relationship with 17–18, 38, 59–60, 84–5, 106*fig.*
as team members 86–7
coaching 87–8
collaboration
awards for 9, 54–7
case study: Van Leeuwen Ice Cream: How a fresh design increased sales 4–8, 6–8*ill.*
creative values and 20, 21*fig.*
and in-house teams 53–4
importance of 1–2, 3–4, 34
and introverts 62
colleagues, as mentors 95
collectives, freelance 86
communication 14–15, 33, 62, 65–6, 106
with clients 31, 34–5, 42
creative values and 21*ill.*
importance of 18–19
communities, creative
case study: Make a Mark: Building Community by Giving Back 99–106, 101–3*ill.*, 106*fig.*
cultivating 108–9
mentorship 106
online 97–8
peer groups 94–5
professional organizations 96
skill sharing 99
teams as 93–4
community agreements 16
consultancies 27, 42
copywriters 17, 84–6
creative directors, role of 16–17
Creative Reaction Lab 99
CreativeMorning 97
creators, individual 2
Crosby, Theo 28
culture 14, 21*fig.*
Curtis, Kristen 84–6

Dall, Phil 84
Davis, Meredith 9, 20
deadlines 87
Design Bridge agency 78–83, 83*fig.*

design challenges 99
"Design Futures" report 9, 10, 19
Design Management Institute 3
Design Values Index (DVI) 3
designers, role of 17
DevChat platform 97
development, creative 1, 60, 99
Dewey, Vanessa 3–4
digital technology 4, 9, 60–1, 87, 94 *see also* social media; websites
directors, role of 16–17
diversity 11–14, 107
Doyle Dane Bernbach agency 2–3
Drymalski, Tom 36–8
Dublin, use in bottle packaging design *see* Jameson Whiskey

education, professional 98
effectiveness 18–20, 90–1
efficiency 61
Emans, Denielle J. and Kelly M. Murdoch-Kitt: *Intercultural Collaboration and Design* 14, 18, 19
entrepreneurship 88–9, 108
equity 11–13, 16, 107
Erb, Veronica: *How to Stop Steamrolling and Start Thinking Together* 62
Espinoza, Junior 113–14
exercises
finding a creative mentor 110–12
tracking your work habits 90–1
types of agency 47–9
understanding an in-house brand 69–70
"Eyes Up" campaign *see* Make a Mark "Eyes Up" campaign

Facebook 97 *see also* social media
Faust, William 53–4
fees 45, 72–3, 88
Ferguson, Dan 46
film *see* animation
Fletcher, Alan 28
flexibility 20, 35–6, 63
Flourish online platform 97
Forbes, Colin 28
freelance working
benefits of 71

case study: Jameson Whiskey: Collaborating as a freelance illustrator 78–83, 79*ill.*, 81–3*ill.*, 83*fig.*
clients 84, 86–7
coaching 87–8
collectives 86
direct-to-client 73
effective habits 72, 90–1
lifestyle 89
personal creative style 74–5, 80
professional networks 75–7
rates 72–3
teams 10, 66, 71–2, 84–7, 114
workflows 77–8

Google LLC 107
Grange, Kenneth 28
Graphic Artists Guild 96
Greene, Helen 43–4, 46
Greenhaus GFX studio 43–4, 46
Groove Jones creative technology company 46

Half, Robert 72
Han, Joseph 5
Hands Down! agency 54
Harmon, Brooke 31–5
Harris, Thomas 65–8, 107
Hayman, Luke 28
hierarchy 30
Hische, Jessica: Daily Drop Cap website 76
'Hopes and Fears' activity 16
Hornsby, Sue 56

IBM 16, 19, 62–4
inclusion 12, 13
individual creators 2
in-house teams 10, 45, 51, 65–8, 114
    case study: Inside Out Awards: Celebrating In-House Creative Work 54–8, 57–8*ill.*, 59*fig.*
    challenges and opportunities 65, 68
    collaboration 53–4, 61–2
    communication 65–6
    development 68
    goals 59–60
    perceptions of 64–5
    processes 65–6
    types of work 60–1
    value of 51–3
    work/life balance 67
Inside Out Awards: Pentland Brands "Be Part of It" campaign 54–8, 57–8*ill.*, 59*fig.*
integrated teams 53–4
interns, role of 17

Jameson Whiskey, limited edition bottle packaging design 78–83, 79*ill.*, 81–3*ill.*, 83*fig.*
Jantos, Jackie 53
Jarvis, Paul 71–2, 87
    Company of One 88–9
Jen, Natasha 5, 29, 46

Kobet, Deanna 100
Kurlansky, Mervyn 28

Lack, Allyson 23, 35–6
Ladies Wine and Design 96
Lamar University 60
leadership 20, 29, 33–5
learning, online 98
LGBTQ+ creatives 107
Life Cereal advertising campaign 3
lifestyle 21*ill.*, 22, 89
logos 6*ill.*, 37
Lundberg, Daniel 80
Lupton, Ellen 18, 19

Make a Mark "Eyes Up" campaign 93, 99–106, 101–3*ill.*, 106*fig.*
management team, roles of 17–18
Manglapus, Rhea 5
marketing 27, 31, 43
matrix model 24–5, 25*ill.*
Mattel, Inc. 3–4
McDonald, Georgina 5
McKinley, Angelica 4, 60–1
McLemore, Daniel 51, 60
McNeese, Evie 100
mentors 85, 94, 95, 106–8, 110–12, 113
models, organizational 24, 25*ill.*
modular systems 61
money 88–9 *see also* fees
motion graphics 27, 43–4, 46 *see also* animation

motivation 30
multi-disciplinary structures 47
Mumford, Gwendolyn 65–8

Nagpurkar, Veda 31–5
National Equity Project 16
National Industries for the Blind 87
networks, professional 75–7, 93–4, 108
New York Times 4, 60–1
New Yorker magazine 38, 39*ill.*
Newman, Daniel 62
Newton, Rose 106
Nowitski, Dirk 46
NPR Digital Design Media Group 62, 87
NSPCC (National Society for the Prevention of Child Cruelty) 56

Obenauer, Mark 93
Obenauer, Sarah 93, 99–100
O'Bryan, Devin 19, 61, 62–4
office spaces 29
OH Partners agency 31–5, 32*fig.*
Olivo, Sarah 100, 104
Ologie consultancy 53
online communities 97–8, 108
Only Child design company 84–6
organizational models 24, 25*fig.*
organizations, professional 94, 96–7, 110

packaging design *see* Jameson Whiskey, bottle packaging design; Van Leeuwen ice cream rebranding
Park, Ji 5
partnerships 86
Pentagram agency 4–8, 23, 28–30, 31, 36, 46–7
Pentland Brands *see* Inside Out Awards: Pentland Brands "Be Part of It" campaign
pitching 77, 79, 80
'plug and play' agency model 52–3
'pod' agency model 8*fig.*, 24, 26*fig.*, 47
podcasts 108
Polaroid advertising campaign 3
portfolios 74, 77, 114
pricing *see* fees
Principle agency 23–4, 35–6

production companies 27, 43
professional organizations 94, 96–7, 108, 110
profit sharing 28–9
project managers 17–18
Public Relations Society of America (PRSA) 96
Publicis agency 24, 36–41

quality control 77–8

Rae, Jeneanne 3
Rand, Paul 3
rebranding 4–8
record keeping 73
remote working 73, 89
Rezac, Jen 100
R/GA agency 46–7
Rising Tide Society 97
roles, team members 16–18

safety, creative 11
salaries 72–3 *see also* fees
Scher, Paula 23
scrum masters, role of 18
'Second Life' Tennessee program *see* Make a MArk "Eyes Up" Campaign
Sexton, Emma 52, 54, 55*ill.*
Shannon, Kathleen 42, 108–10
signage 8*ill.*
Simpson, Steve 74–5, 76, 77–80, 83*fig.*
skills, creative 98–9
Slack online platform 61, 97
smartphone apps 9, 37, 40*ill.*, 46
social media 34, 75–6, 97, 98, 110, 111
Society of Illustrators 96
software 63, 64, 97
solo working 62
Spotify 53
Sterner, Maggy 87–8
stock market 3
strategy, creative 2, 17, 31, 42, 51, 61
Street, Tara 42
structure
  agencies 24, 28–31, 32*fig.*, 45
  teams 8*ill.*, 41*fig.*, 59*fig.*
students 96, 98, 108, 112
studios 27, 28

style, personal 74–5
supervisors 94–5

Table of Content production company 43
talent, creative 30
team structure 8*ill.*, 32*ill.*, 41*fig.*, 59*fig.*, 106*fig.*
teams 33–4, 62 *see also* freelance working; in-house teams
   art director/copywriter 84–6
   definitions 10
   diversity in 11–14
   freelancer/client 86–7
   integration 53–4
   roles within 16–18
   types of 114
teamwork 1–2, 20, 24
technology *see* digital technology
Thompson, Emily 108
time management 87, 90–1
Toast Masters 97
Todoca, Ramona 11
Toppins, Aggie 2
toys, campaigns for 3

traditional agency model 26, 45
trust 11, 85, 87
typography 78

universities 108 *see also* students
"Unlock New York" *see* Citi Bike campaign
Unofficial Hand Lettering Society of Silver Spring 98

value, adding 52
values 20–2, 21*ill.*, 114
Van Leeuwen ice cream rebranding 4–8, 6–8*ill.*, 29
video marketing 43
Volkswagen advertising campaign 3

Walters, Kelly 13
Warner, Frances 104
waterfall processes 64
websites 76–7, 87
Weintraub advertising agency 3
women 23, 84, 107
work spaces 54, 72
workflows 64, 77–8
work/life balance 64, 67, 68, 71, 89